Animated N

Selected Poems b

1989 - 2

COYPU PUBLICATIONS

1

A Bestiary - an Animal Alphabet…1993

"Richard Bonfield is a poet with an acute ear and a sensitive response to language, with the happy ability to use words like building blocks in creations which come fresh to our eyes. In a Bestiary he is revealed as a witty verbal comedian; an ebullient cartoonist in words."
Charles Roberts, Former Literary Editor: The Eastern Daily Press

"To a true bestiarist ..from a part time one."
Marina Warner: Dedication in Mermaids in the Basement

"Richard Bonfield's A-Z of animals is beautifully and lovingly expressed. Highly descriptive and injected with moments of fun, each animal emerges with a character and personality of its own."
Judith Pearson, Actress and reader: Poetry Please, BBC Radio 4

Swan for all Seasons...1997

"Swan for all seasons is exquisite..... Congratulations...!"
Elspeth Barker, Reviewer: The Independent on Sunday

"Swan for all Seasons is a beautiful...beautiful book."
Martin Holroyd, Editor: Poetry Monthly

Swan for all Seasons ."is a delightful book, both for Richard Bonfield's poems and Carol Turner's and David Atkinson's drawings."
Len McCarthy, Editor: Candelabrum

"Swan for all Seasons is excellent and well worth all your time and trouble. It will be getting a fine review in H.Q."
(See below....)

"This is very much a book to settle down with next to a warm winter fire-place. It will reassure you that Spring and Summer do exist and that love is possible and the world is full of hope. The book is beautifully produced by Coypu Publications and is dedicated to support of The Wildfowl and Wetlands Trust....
This is a book which, rarely in these times deserves every penny of its asking price."
Kevin Bailey, Editor: The Haiku Quarterly

"The swan in this well produced book is Bonfield with his keen observation of Nature from poetry's quiet lake."
Ai Li, Editor: Still

"He gets close to the love of nature without undue sentimentality. This book would be a delightful present for a lover of wildlife - even if they had not yet developed a taste for modern poetry..!"
Margaret Pain, Reviewer: Iota

Supporting the Wildfowl and Wetlands Trust Richard Bonfield's attractive second collection is a journey through the seasons of the year, and life, and is beautifully and delicately Illustrated. There are many and varied snapshot poems.. "Every so often a poem shines a torch." he says in *The Museum of Love* and many of these shed an illuminating insight into Richard's perceptive mind. There are several gems - such as *Bonsai Garden*..."In this morning dewdrop/Your whole garden/Shines... dip into it again and again and you are rewarded with riches."
Jeremy Duffield, Assistant Editor: Poetry Nottingham International

Menagerie - another Animal Alphabet...2004
The General Public have their say..!

"Congratulations.. A fabulous achievement...! Hippo made me laugh hugely..!"
Alison Towndrow: Leicester

"Congratulations on a superb anthology..!"
Denise Margaret Hargrave: Yorkshire

"It is a brilliant book..! It is a wonderful book..!"
Gerald and Sheila Hampshire: Yorkshire

"Your poems are beautiful. I have never read anything like them before. They are all like fresh drops in the eye which make you see differently. I know that this is a horrible *teachery* thing to say (I'm an ex - English teacher currently doing basic skills with learning difficulties - which is 10 x more fun and satisfying) but I think your book is 100% perfect for kids; they are fun, meaning something - accessible, you name it. They should be more widely read."
P.S "If you do readings/performances could you let me have a copy of any programmes...? We could get over to Leicester from here... Thanks.."
Sue Adamson: Derbyshire

"Congratulations..! Excellent poems and pleasing images combine to form a charming picture of the magical creatures which share this beautiful planet of ours."
Margaret Munro Gibson: Cheshire

"Many thanks for the book. It is quite excellent.. The book is a good mixture of straight poems, comedy and fantasy, forcing one to use both intellect and imagination."
Audrey Goaley: Sutton Coldfield

"My first impressions are one of delight and awe...! The presentation - with the fabulous illustrations make it a book that is ....*good to the touch*...It is a real treat to open it and discover world upon world rising before my eyes, the world of the flea, for instance and the world of the giraffe....to move from the ridiculous to the sublime...! The world of the naturalist's eye tempered with that of the mythologist's mystery seem to juxtapose quite harmoniously."
Caroline Gill: Wales

"My most sincerest congratulations to you. Menagerie is a joy to read. The book has been beautifully produced, the illustrations are entirely appropriate for the mood of your poems and I trust it will be a great success for you."
Eileen Hubbard: Leicester

"Many thanks once again for your super book of poems.!"
Mary McClean: Norwich

"Many thanks for your dazzling Menagerie,...beautiful poems full of fun, imagination and reality... and such apposite images.."
Shirley Turner: Bristol

"A stunning volume. What can I say about the poems themselves apart, from what I have already mentioned in my letters? I marvel at their originality and insight, what Gerard Manley Hopkins might have recognized as *inscape*. if he'd been lucky enough to read them. Thank you very much dear Richard for such an inexhaustible cornucopia of Treasures. I hope I live to see *'Scarecrow' in* the fullness of time."
Dorothy Aitken, aged 94: West Sussex

"Congratulations..! Your new birth is Big...Bonny... and STRONG..!!!."
Claire Riggall, former editor Poetry Nottingham: Radcliffe on Trent

"Congratulations..! Menagerie is superb, as I knew it would be...!"
Shelagh Nugent Retiring Editor, Reach: The Wirral

"Dear Mr Bonfield. Thank you for sending me Menagerie. It is marvellous for dipping into, full of surprises and verses that amuse."
Carol Hughes, Court Green, North Tawton: Devon

Reviews for Menagerie continued…
The Critics have their say…!

"The follow up to his well received 1998 collection *A Bestiary - an Animal Alphabet* is a delightful collection of animal poems in the tradition of alphabet sequences that encapsulates the animal kingdom, both real and imagined, in an impressive variety of poetic forms. All animal life is here from the ant eater *The Dyson of the termite groves to Zooplankton… phantasmagoric bubbleflies*. These poems possess a delightful deftness of touch as well as a wry sense of humour, combining traditional style with a twenty - first century imagination. There are some enjoyable responses and A thoroughly enjoyable read for animal and poetry lovers alike."
Jane Bluett, Regional Co-ordinator of the National Association for the Teaching of English.

"Richard Bonfield's new *Menagerie - another Animal Alphabet* is an almost perfect mix of poetry and illustration. The poetry has Mr Bonfield's trademark confection of energy, wit and the charm of rhyme. I have said before that he is the modern day Lear - and I stand by that. There is good nature, joy and celebration of life in almost every poem…. And a sly humour.
Here's *Barbara Cartland's Flamingo*.…

> *The flamingo is so very pink*
> *She blushes when she stoops to drink*
>
> *She's Barbara Cartland's favourite bird*
> *That mistress of the rosebud word*
>
> *And when she flies into the sun*
> *The colours of her wing tips run*
>
> *To paint a soft carnation dusk*
> *That's filled with sugar coated lust.*

This is not a poetry for the university academic, or the London critic - it is not angst-ridden nor often serious, but I have a feeling it says more about the world than many a more *highfalutin* work, and I suspect is going to endure - partly because it will enter the imagination, memory and affection of several generations of children. The animal illustrations are taken from Victorian engravings and woodcuts.

Here's the opening of *Rook*

The rook
Has a black intelligence

An avian hell's angel
He loves his tribe

For he is the biker of the Autumn skies......

This collection will make the perfect first book of poetry for any child, and cheer up any depressed or care worn adult. It is a breath of fresh air. Beautifully printed and bound, it also proves that when a poet makes his/her book a true labour of love, they are half - way there… Sales of Menagerie will help to support the work of the British Trust for Conservation Volunteers..
How many more reasons do you need to buy a book……?"
Kevin Bailey, Editor: the Haiku Quarterly

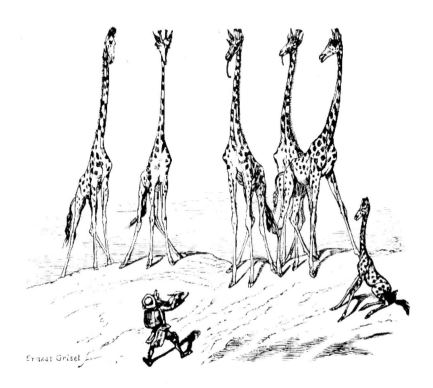

Ernest Grisel

Copyright

First published in 2010 by
Coypu Publications
18 Poppy Close
The Maltings
Leicester
LE2 6UR
e mail richardbonfieldpoet@talktalk.net
with the help of The Natural Animators

Poems Typeset in Futura Light
Front cover typeset in Sylfaen
All Rights Reserved
ISBN 0 9521016 3 7

Printed by Waypoint Print Solutions
10 Santareen Road
Long Stratton
Norwich
NR15 2NZ
Tel: 01508 531899
Fax: 0158 532433

Acknowledgements

My thanks go to the respective editors of the following Magazines/Websites/ Anthologies in which the majority of these poems first appeared or were subsequently re-printed/ anthologized/broadcast.

The Acorn Anthology of Contemporary Haiku, BBC Wildlife Magazine, The Bluechrome Anthology of Contemporary Poetry, The Born Free Website and Podcast, By the Winter Fires, Candelabrum, Dawntreader, Earthlove, Envoi, Exile, First Time, The Forward Press, The Haiku Quarterly, Helicon, Iota, Krax, Littoral, Moonstone, Outposts, Pagan Dawn, Pentacle, Peer Poetry, Pennine Ink, Pennine Platform, Poetry Monthly, Places within Reach, Poetry Nottingham, Poetry Nottingham International, Poet Tree, Radio 4's Natural History Programme, Reach, The best of Reach 2008, The Red Candle Anthology of Late Twentieth Century Poetry, Spiked, Still, Still on Line, Triumph Herald, The Twin Towers Memorial Website, TVP, Weyfarers and ZLR.

Horse Whisperer, Night Thoughts of an Oak Tree, Chaucer's Bluebells, Dormouse Triptych, After Cerebral Aneurism, Zooplankton, The Beautiful Alphabet & The Tortworth Chestnut were all First Prize Winners in The Reach Poetry competition.
The poem Haiku for a Robin was first broadcast on Radio 4's Natural History Programme in 1993.
Turin Shroud was chosen as one of the top 100 poems by The Forward Press in 2000.
Zooplankton was a prize winner in The BBC Wildlife Magazine Poet of the Year Competition in 2002.
Daddy Long Legs was the only poem commended in the adult category of the same competition in 2009.

Many Guardian Spirits have befriended me along the way. I have only made it thus far by standing on the shoulders and abusing the hospitality of others - often equally impecunious but, nevertheless far more generous and less self-serving than "my very humble and ingratiating self". I have only made it thus far "with a lot of help from my friends" and I owe you all a debt of gratitude which can never - in many cases literally be repaid..! You should all have your name in lights; but this would require a book in itself.
However I certainly wouldn't be where I am today without the help and critical encouragement of Claire Riggall who, in her former guise as Claire Piggott first began accepting my poems for Poetry Nottingham in the early 1990's and I am most grateful to her for agreeing to write the Introduction. She it was who suggested that I write an animal alphabet in the first place calling it 'A Bestiary', after the mediaeval Natural History books and without her support and encouragement it is unlikely that any of this

would ever have seen the light of day....!

I am also eternally grateful to Keith Smith and Maria Guerten, talented potters and artists both who kept open house for me at their studio in Elm Hill Norwich and became in some sense my spiritual parents. Keith it was who introduced me to David Sainsbury the eminent Cambridge vet and don who became my patron for the next decade. David sadly died a few years ago now, but during the period of our creative acquaintance he was unstinting in his weekly correspondence and encouragement. He it was who provided the wherewithal for the reprint of A Bestiary and without his good humour and generosity of spirit I have little doubt that Menagerie would not have seen the light of day.

I look back with great fondness to our twice yearly meetings at The George at Stamford with his charming wife Ursula and am glad that I am able to include the poem *Summerlands* in the present volume as a token of my affection for them and their extended family.

Fortune smiled on me again last year when the poetic baton was taken up by Virginia McKenna the famous and much loved actress who, with her husband Bill Travers founded the charity Born Free. Virginia was given a copy of A Bestiary a few years ago and was much taken with the poem *The Beautiful Alphabet* which seemed to her to sum up all she had been striving for.

Her son Will who now runs the charity was equally moved and last year they finally managed to track me down and do me the great honour of asking me to be their Poet in Residence. I am both excited and delighted to have been elevated to such a position and the present volume which supports the work of the Born Free foundation is the first fruit of what I trust will be a rewarding collaboration on behalf of our em-battled planet.

Thanks must also be extended to Celia Nicholls, Born Free's editorial Head of Publications, David Jay (Senior Programmes Officer - Field Conservation) her partner and her daughter Tabitha for their wonderful hospitality during my visit last year and to Mike Dooley, Joanne Bartholomew, Claire Stanford and David Pledger all mem-bers of the Born Free crew who are working tirelessly on the planet's behalf.

Virginia McKenna introduced me to her great friend Pollyanna Pickering, the inter-nationally acclaimed wildlife artist and I was lucky enough to be sent as Born Free's representative to the opening night of Pollyanna's exhibition celebrating the 25th anni-versary of Born Free's Foundation late last Summer. Pollyanna had spent some time with her daughter Anna - Louise making sketches of the wildlife in Virginia's reserves in Africa and had also produced some amazing images of Elsa inspired by Joy Adamson's books with some of the proceeds of the exhibition going towards the es-tablishment of Born Free's newest reserve in Ethiopia and I was lucky enough to forge a relationship with both Pollyanna and Anna - Louise, which was strengthened with subsequent visits to their beautiful home just outside Matlock in Derbyshire and I am delighted to say that Pollyanna has now done me the great honour of allowing me to use one of her latest Kingfisher paintings as the cover of the present volume.

I have included a brief biography of Pollyanna by way of thanks for her great generosity of spirit and to introduce her to the few people out there who may not be familiar with her work.

The present volume would not have seen the light of day in its present form without the prodigious efforts of Terry Butteriss my graphic designer without whom I am nothing but a headless chicken…! He has, as always gone beyond the call of duty and the look and feel of Animated Nature is in no small measure down to his efforts, although I must confess that I did spend some time schooling him in the art of seeing the world through Victorian spectacles…! To his great credit he took my advice on board and has subsequently outstripped me with his verve and creative invention .He is kind, generous and attentive to a fault and his passion for lists helped me through the creation of the Contents and the Index, something which would have taxed my less orderly imagination. We have spent many a Saturday morning shivering on the decking outside the Old Crown (mine hosts, Gary and Kerry) at Wigston, our favoured watering hole and much of the look and feel of the book was sketched out here, aided and abetted by jovial criticism from *"the usual suspects.....!"*

My Family and other Animals have as always been supportive of my endeavours and Jani Somani and Richard Davies our wonderful next door neighbours have been towers of strength . No one could have truer friends and their help and support, especially with the planning of The Launch Party has been inspirational.

The whole journey could never have been accomplished or indeed considered without the aid of all my friends from The Wind's Twelve Quarters and I would like to finish this section by pausing once again to thank all the guardian spirits along the way who have befriended me. This book is dedicated to all of you.

Last, but by no means least I would like to reach my hand across the river Styx and shake the hands of all the largely anonymous Victorian engravers who have helped to bring my poems to life over the last 20 years.

Ever since the fortuitous discovery of Knight's Pictorial Museum of Animated Nature at the eleventh hour on the eve of the publication of A Bestiary and the equally fortuitous discovery of Knight's Pictorial History of England on the eve of the publication of Swan for all Seasons my work has been aided and abetted by the labours of these formidably talented artists.

Each new collection has generally led to further artistic discoveries and this time round I would like to single out for special mention British Birds in their Haunts by the Rev W.C. John's, the David Attenborough/Bellamy of his day and more precisely the earlier editions of this work before the advent of dismal black and white photography destroyed the engraver's magic lantern. I am also indebted to the work of Ernest Griset the great Victorian anthropomorphic illustrator whose oeuvre I discovered so fortuitously at the eleventh hour, courtesy of my wonderfully eccentric friend Jeannie Arbuckle. Griset's work graces the bookends i.e. the material at the front and back of the collection and I am delighted to have discovered a kindred spirit of whom I was previously unaware.

Andy 'Art Bailey' my animal alphabet calligrapher contributed the image of yours truly in the Director's chair on the Dramatis Personae page and he is, I like to think, the inheritor of Griset's mantle.

The illustrations in this collection were taken from.......

Knight's Pictorial Museum of Animated Nature
Knight's Pictorial History of England in 2 volumes
Winner's in Life's Race by Arabella Buckley
The Water Babies by Charles Kingsley
The Forest Trees of Britain by the Rev W.C. John's
Flowers of the Field by the Rev W.C. John's
British Birds in their Haunts by the Rev W.C. John's
Familiar Wild Birds by W. Swaysland
The Scripture Picture Book
The works of Ernest Griset

Other images were found courtesy of the Internet
Posthumous thanks to their respective Victorian illustrators.

The Natural Animators

Listed below are all those who have contributed fiscally to the genesis of the collection. This particular set of clippings from the Bonfield archive would never have been spliced into anything approaching a coherent poetic film without their help and I am truly grateful for their pecuniary input. Many of those listed have been fellow travellers for many years, whilst others listed have been more recent Guardian Spirits who have befriended me along life's highway. Many expected this collection to be out a year ago, but patience is a virtue and I am thankful that my many friends and supporters possess it in abundance......!

Paul Amphlett, Anon, Jeannie Arbuckle, Marie Bakewell, Richard Barsby, Bernard O'Brien, Beryl and Victor Bonfield, Christopher Bonfield, Joan Bonfield, Jim and Emma Buchanan, Dick and Margaret Bultitude, Janine Crowcombe, Richard Davies, Diane and Peter Eaton, Lucy Ellis, Gina Finnegan, Christine Fletcher, Valerie Flatman, Emma Fraser, Wendy Gaston, Anthony Gilbert, Caroline and David Gill, Audrey Goaley, Stephen and Yvonne Goaley, Shirley Goddard, Patrick Goodall, Cathy Grindrod, Denise Margret Hargrave and Tony, Christine Hewson, Annie Holgate, Eileen Hubbard, Janet and John Hubbard, Gwen and Peter Johnson, Lloyd and Sara Johnson, Claire Knight, Joanna Mackintosh, Malvern St James O.G.A., Wolf Malucha, Judith Pearson, Deena Marvin, Roy McLean, Mollie Muetzel, Roz Myhill, Minka Nicholson, Cecilia Physic, Rosemary and Barrie Raynor, Claire Riggall, Raymond Riley, Pam Russell, Anthony Sainsbury, Ursula Sainsbury, Tricia Saxton, Diana Scholefield, Joy Shaw, Perminder Singh, Sheila and Peter Solly, Jani Somani, Lamorna Spink, Ann Stallard, Susan Stewart, Pip Storer, Russell Storer, Michael Tebbutt, Jenny and Tony Tillyer, Alison Towndrow, Veryan and David, Virginia Travers, Shirley Turner and Ian Wright.

During the gestation of Animated Nature Dorothy Aitken, my oldest fan died at the age of 94 as did the much loved poet and supporter of my work Margaret Munro Gibson, and Bernard O' Brian, my great friend from Cover days in Norwich all those years ago and Pete Brown and the lovely Ellie from Rainbow Wholefood days in a Fine City.

I would also to remember Judith Pearson the actress and reader on Radio 4's Poetry Please who did so much to help me in the early days and who sadly died of Alzheimer's several years ago, Warren Sperry the ASDA porter—a truly loveley man who passed away last year and Richard Boyes our former ASDA security supreme who departed this earthly life just before Christmas 2009.

It is a great shame that they did not live to see the fruits of my labours but I am sure they are both smiling on me from above.

The Beautiful Alphabet: *For Virginia McKenna, Will Travers, the Born Free Team and adults everywhere*

"What were Tigers...?" said the child
"They were muscled furnaces" said the mother
"They burned through Darjeeling
They had tails like a daisy chain of bumble bees
They had paws like the columns of Solomon's temple
They were strong and gentle and could not be humbled
And they weaved themselves though the weft of the jungle"
"And what were Elephants....?" said the child
"They were skin houses" said the father
"They had lovely hosepipes they waved at the moon
They looked like your uncle in a rumpled room
They had ears that flapped like sails in the rain
They had tusks that curved like prows of flame"
"And Dolphins...?" said the child
"They were sea-planes" said the mother
"Slip-streamed by time
They were Aquanauts hunting the Golden Fleece
They were sailing harbingers of surf-smiling peace"
"And where have they gone...?" said the child
"They have buried themselves in our imagination"
Said the mother
"And the Alphabet is chrome and steel
And the plains are empty and the jungles fields
For the world had no need of irrelevant things
Gossamer condors with sun-scraping wings
So they put all the creatures in a chromium ark
And fired it into the star-crusted evening
And now - on some far distant planet
The Tigers are burning
The Dolphins are flying with unbridled mirth
And the Elephants are waving their lovely hosepipes
At the sad and empty earth"
"Can we go there sometime" said the child
"And learn The Beautiful Alphabet....?"
"Sometime..." said the mother and father
With tearful sighs........
Then they switched out the light in their daughter's eyes.

Introduction

It was in late 1990 that Richard's first packet of poems hit my desk. As Editor of Poetry Nottingham I was used to the standard fare of the small presses — love, the miracle of birth, the misery of unemployment, the bereaved - as well as to the unusual and even outstanding which (I like to think) found their way into the magazine. As I unfolded and read Elephant that morning I knew I was hearing a new voice with something important to say. From the awe of "The great Earth Whale....Calling to the Planet/to save itself from idle pleasures" to the deep anger and compassion for the ivory trinkets "That litter the mantelpiece of Africa" I knew I had struck gold.

During the next two years I included at least one poem of Richard's in every issue of PN. Eventually it became apparent that there was an animal poem for almost every letter of the alphabet and I suggested that he should compile a collection and call it *A Bestiary,* like the Mediaeval books of beast Fables. The rest is history. *A Bestiary: an Animal Alphabet* was published in 1993 and a second impression came out in 1999. Meanwhile *Swan for all Seasons* appeared in 1997 and in the new century the output continued with *Menagerie* – a companion piece to *A Bestiary* in 2004..

Animated Nature - Selected Poems 1989-2009 is an exciting new project. It is a distillation of all the poems written during the last twenty years. There is no room for anything less than good and in my view some of the latest work is as good as anything previously collected, taking influences from poetry in English from ancient to modern, from Celtic life and legends, the Old and New Testaments and Egyptology — not by any means a comprehensive list — as well as from the natural world in all its manifestations.

Some of these poems hurl themselves spontaneously from the page, untroubled by pauses or stops. This is of course an illusion which takes no account of the painstaking process of crafting, rewriting, revising, trying out and general agonising. But the best of them still hurl themselves into the reader's consciousness and lodge there, with their impassioned cries at man's inhumanity to man, animal and our planet. What other imagination could have described in *The Passing of the Buffalo* how once the vast herds "swarmed on the Western plains/Like deafening shag pile?"

It isn't just all "nature poetry". There are topical and occasional responses also, and personal loves and griefs, recording some of the desperately sad and unfair things that just happen to people, lightly done in *After Cerebral Aneurism* — She's Heather still/But watered down? Imprisoned in her dressing gown. Her book has torn its central spine/The pages fall out all the time. You will find light relief, occasional rudeness, in - character pieces and haiku. Above all, from these pages you will receive the gift of seeing something in a new way: when I first read "smash open the book of time/And Archaeopteryx is dancing/Throwing out limbs of feathered limestone" it dawned on me that my days of regarding a fossil as a lump of rock were over. I hope new readers will enjoy many such "aha" moments.

Animated Nature is an exciting project for another reason. Last year Richard became Poet in Residence to the Born Free foundation: his poems can now be heard on its website and Virginia McKenna has recorded *The Beautiful Alphabet,* the poem which concluded the first collection, *A Bestiary* and sparked her interest in his work. In every sense Richard is on a stunning new path and after beetling away at his poems for over two decades has gone global. This is a marriage made in heaven - A Foundation dedicated to the aim of eliminating animal exploitation and a poet's voice to give it an extra and extraordinary dimension.

Claire Riggall   XV

The Kingfisher, The Holographic Paradigm and The Perennial Philosophy

Until quite recently debates on the nature of Science and Religion have concentrated on their differences by maintaining that they are, basically 2 different approaches to reality, Science concentrating on the What? Whilst Religion concentrates on the Why.?

Now many people - it seems to me are still mired in this outlook, unaware that a seismic shift has taken place in the last 50 years which holds out the promise of the marriage of these two different approaches to reality. Reality - after all is one.

On the frontiers of science this debate has been carried out by the late David Bohm - former Professor of Theoretical Physics at Birbeck College London with his theory of the implicate order, Fritjof Capra, the theoretical physicist, perhaps best known for his ground breaking work The Tao of Physics as well as books such as The Turning Point and Belonging to the Universe and Rupert Sheldrake the maverick biologist, noted for his theory of morphogenetic fields whilst, on the religious front the Dalai Lama, Lama Govinda and father Bede Griffiths author of The Golden String who moved from Christian monasticism to Eastern asceticism, before uniting and finding the middle way have all been instrumental in fermenting and sustaining the creative dialogue.

The central vision that informs the emergent science of The Holographic Paradigm is that the world - in the ground of its unutterable being is the same unutterable world of unitive mystics such as Meister Eckhart, the great Zen masters and the writers of The Upanishads. The universe it appears, as the mystics of The Perennial Philosophy have always taught us is both intellectually and intuitively one. This vision, as far as science is concerned is best captured in the holographic images created by lasers where it is known that the part of every image contains enough information to recreate the whole. As far as the mystics are concerned this knowledge was already contained in The Upanishads where the pearls of Shiva's necklace are conceived as reflecting and reproducing the light of the eternal ground such that each pearl reflects and reproduces the light of the whole of creation.

As far as biology is concerned we now know that each cell of our body contains the potential to produce the whole so this perennial idea is inter - disciplinary and is continually being confirmed by new discoveries on the leading edge of thought.

Bohm's theory of the implicate order holds out the promise that the universe as we see it from the confines of our bounded ego is actually only the explicate unfolding of an implicate order within which everything is, reacts with and reflects everything else.

In musical terms the external, explicate order is but a marvellous variation on Paganini's original theme which permeates the work like a melodic watermark. Held up to the light of mystical awareness one sees that everything is, in reality a manifestation of the implicate order of creation known in necessarily paradoxical terms as the Sound of Silence or the Divine Ground of Being.

Quantum physics, first developed in the 1920's and 30's has already shown us that we cannot separate the observer from the observed and - whilst science has not yet postulated, let alone been able to prove that the world of the quantum applies at the Newtonian level the mystic has always maintained that this is the case and - as a poet and would be mystic this has certainly been my humble experience i.e. the universe as a given does not always operate as if it is 'out there' but, sometimes as if it is an extension of my unbounded self. I have, for example had many instances in my life of synchronicity, wish fulfilment and meaningful coincidences which lead me to suppose that there is a higher level of order in the universe which reveals connections between disparate material phenomena that are not detectable by science, although they make sense in a mystical universe in which quantum effects such as non locality operate in our everyday world. For example, most of the time - as a particulate observer I experience the world as differentiated; however, when in a wave - like state the world becomes more permeable and I can walk, if only for a timeless moment or two through the wardrobe - or Alice's Looking Glass mirror.

This sense becomes particularly acute when in the process of poetic creation or when walking in a natural landscape such that when people talk of being at one with nature they are, albeit unwittingly pointing to a truth which can be experienced in sacramental time.

Most of the time we walk through nature as a differentiated particulate observer but, on those rare 'magic lantern' days we enter into a more interactive landscape in which the underlying unity of the cosmic ground is made manifest i.e. "Touch a flower and you trouble a star."

To produce a 'concrete' example of the phenomenon I remember a beautiful Autumn day a couple of years ago when I walked the same stretch of canal I have walked for the last 40 years in that lower light so beautifully captured by Samuel Palmer which only this season brings. I had been hoping - as usual to see a kingfisher and my hope, although seemingly unfounded in any rational way was high. The light was preternatural, almost ethereal and I did feel as If I was moving through a transfigured landscape; however I saw nothing untoward, apart from the light and upon returning was just about to pass the lock keeper's cottage and wend my way up through the field when I saw the kingfisher, which I have always regarded as my totemic animal on the lock gate. It was almost as if I had to give up all rational expectation before my wish was granted; however there it was in all its transfigured glory and as I watched in amazement it took off and darted from side to side up the evening canal until it was caught up in the skirts of the setting sun.

This unexpected benediction was like the answer to a Zen koan or Jesus' instruction that "whosoever shall lose their life for my sake shall find it."

I felt that I had stood, if only for a moment before Blake's Doors of Perception in a landscape painted by Samuel Palmer and described by Thomas Traherne and I felt that I had just experienced Wordsworth's sense of something more deeply interfused… which rolls through all things.

At the end of the day I had seen a kingfisher, but it was no ordinary kingfisher and it was no ordinary day. It was a day when I saw Annie Dillard's "Tree with the lights" and gazed through the window of eternity.

Richard Bonfield c 2006
First published in Littoral: Summer Solstice 2006

Reading List

The Perennial Philosophy: Edited with an introduction by Aldous Huxley
The Holgraphic Paradigm and other Paradoxes: Edited by Ken Wilbur
Dialogues with Scientists and Sages:Edited by Renee Weber
Wholeness and the Implicate Order: David Bohm
The Golden String: Bede Griffiths
The Tao of Physics: Fritjof Capra
The Turning Point: Fritjof Capra
Belonging to the Universe: Edited by Fritjof Capra
Foundations of Tibetan Mysticism: Lama Govinda
Mysticism: Evelyn Underhill
The Fifth Dimension: John Hick
The Common Experience: J.M Cohen and J. F Phipps
The Varieties of Religious Experience: William James
Maps and Dreams: Hugh Brody
The writings of Meister Eckhart
The Looking Glass Universe: John P.Briggs and F. David Peat
The Upanishads
The works of William Blake
Tintern Abbey:William Wordsworth
The Bhagavad-Gita
Synchronicity: Carl Jung
Pilgrim at Tinker Creek: Annie Dillard

Preface

This collection is entitled Animated Nature in recognition of the great Victorian work of Natural History, Knight's Pictorial Museum of Animated Nature; the equivalent today would be Doring Kindersley's ANIMAL which first appeared towards the end of the 19th century complete with 4000 wood engravings of animals.

My own particular copy was retrieved most fortuitously from Peter Crowe's crammed antiquarian bookshop in Norwich on the eve of the publication of my first collection A Bestiary - an Animal Alphabet which, together with the subsequent discovery of Knight's Pictorial History of England in 2 volumes has helped to both illuminate and invigorate my work ever since.

Other works and Guardian Spirits have appeared as and when required which leads me to believe that the work I am doing is helping to formulate some glorious overarching plan of which I am sometimes dimly and sometimes more brightly aware.

This collection is not intended as a living obituary! My work is not over yet by any means and those looking for a linear procession of Greatest Hits will be sadly disappointed. The intention in this volume has been to gather together all my major preoccupations - the natural world obviously, animals. trees, flowers and stars, alongside other sources of inspiration derived from Nordic, Celtic and Egyptian mythology, together with work inspired by other writers I have admired and events that have occurred in my life which will inevitably strike a chord or chords with a number of readers given the universal nature of the human condition in whatever age we happen to live out our allotted time.

The collection is not themed either, the idea behind it is more along the lines of a miscellany, a walk along a Winter shoreline during which certain pieces may be beach combed and either kept for the mental mantelshelf or, after some consideration thrown back into the glacial depths.. Certain poems have a resonance with the reader which can help to articulate or clarify an emotion or feeling they have not been able to put into words themselves and the poem The Beautiful Alphabet included in this volume certainly had this effect on Virginia McKenna and Will Travers and others will, I hope resonate with the reader and lay old ghosts to rest or help people realise that others too have suffered as they have and lived to tell the tale.

Poets can help people see the world with fresh eyes and they can also make people laugh..! There is a strong comedic element to my work, a scatological sense of the absurd which will, I hope provide a variety of cheerful way stations alongside our more serious paths through Dante's mysterious wood and others will, I hope provide golden compass bearings for those who have temporarily lost their way.

At the end of the day I would like to think that my work as a whole is informed by The Perennial Philosophy and the belief that - when our various journeys are done it is Love that has ultimately informed our thoughts desires and actions, for it is Love that moves the sun and moon, the stars and all the other hemispheres .

Richard Bonfield,
Poppy Close,
Leicester
Remembrance Sunday 2009

Contents

Dramatis Personae

Richard Bonfield

Poems, overall concept
and back cover picture of
Virginia McKenna

Terry Butteriss

Graphic Design, scans,
textual mapping
Contents and Index

Pollyanna Pickering

Front cover painting

Anna - Louise

Inside front and back cover
photographs

The Born Free Team

Virginia McKenna, Will Travers, Celia Nicholls, David Jay, Joanne Bartholomew, Claire Stanford , Mike Dooley and David Pledger. These are the members of the Born Free team most actively involved with the genesis of Animated Nature and the promotion of Richard's work but Born Free is a huge church and there are many other employees and volunteers working tirelessly behind the scenes and across the world for the greater good of both humanity and Animality They know who they are and this book is also dedicated to them.

Written, produced and directed by Richard Bonfield "With a lot of help from my friends."

The Artist

Pollyanna is acclaimed as one of Europe's foremost wildlife artists. The most published artist in the UK, her work sells in over eighty countries world-wide. She is patron of **The Wildlife Art Society International**, and **Derby University** recently awarded her an honorary degree in recognition of her outstanding achievements in the arts. A familiar face on TV, the most recent documentary about her work 'Made in England' was recently broadcast on BBC1

Her paintings will be familiar to most people from her extensive ranges of prints and cards, many commissioned by charities including the **WWF**, **Guide Dogs for the Blind** and the **RSPB**. Pollyanna designs exclusively for **Harrods**, and has painted postage stamps for African countries and First Day Covers for the **Royal Mail**.

Pollyanna, who studied at the **London Central School of Art**, has received many awards for her paintings including a fellowship from the Canada based **Artists for Conservation Foundation**, the **Millennium Trophy** and two gold medals bestowed by **The Wildlife Art Society International**. She has received a commendation for her work in the Arts at the **European Women of Achievement Awards**.

Pollyanna's talks raise funds for her charitable Foundation which supports international conservation and wildlife rescue. Pollyanna also acts as patron of several national charities including **The Badger Trust**, **Naturewatch**, **Raptor Rescue** and the **African/Asian Conservation Trust**.

Painting by Pollyanna Pickering

Dedication

To all the Guardian Spirits along the way who have befriended me

Animated Nature

Selected Poems by Richard Bonfield

1989-2009

One in Many

I am the snake that sheds its skin
To let my soul light glow within

I am the butterfly of love
The Holy Ghost's eternal dove

I am the rainbow bird at dawn
Great Herne the Hunter's ghostly horn

I am the salmon and the seer
The spirit of the running deer

I am the Goddess and the sage
The flame that lights religion's page

I am the Buddha - Atman - Christ
Whichever path you feel is right

For I am everything you see
Creation is my wishing tree

And I am mountain - star and whale
The smile behind creation's veil..

Kingfisher for all Seasons: *For Pollyanna Pickering and Anna - Louise*

The kingfisher
Erupts from charcoal
Like a Zen painting

Brushed to Colour chrome life
He has gathered the stray shades of Summer
Into a loom of Chinese lightning

Caught in the rood of trees
Like stained glass viewed from a spartan season
He roosts underneath the leaking chapel of September

Flies

Like a watercolour fireball on a smoky Autumn evening
Like a splinter of Nirvana in the gentle English snow.

A Local Habitation: *Newton Harcourt, Leicestershire*
For Norman Nicholson and John Clare

I close the time worn kissing-gate
And walk across the furrowed field
To where the old canal winds through
My private - light thronged avenue
And as I turn past Newton lock
I walk along the cleaving path
Where as a child I used to run
Beneath the cowslip of the sun
The heron spreads umbrella wings
And flaps into the springtime sky
The flag iris grow tall and lush
And hug the muddy waterside
The bull rushes - like tall cigars
Are smoking by the wind blown path
And grasshoppers sing match box psalms
Amongst the wild and tangled grass
I stop astride the coppiced stile
And gaze across the pewter sea
To where the sheep and Leicestershire
Roll verdantly away from me
And think of all the dogs who've run
Beside me as the years roll on
And as I stretch beneath the trees
The towpath - dog - canal and me
I think of all the times we've come
The seasons blurring into one
A treading of familiar ways
Lit up by magic lantern days
The fox - one Winter full of drifts
Ice dancing on the frozen Styx

2

The kingfisher in Autumn haze
Perched on the lock gate - all ablaze
And there in Summer's finery
The water vole I used to see
His whiskers weaving through the green
Comes plashing through my memory........
The faithful ducks that always come
Are here - in Springtime paired as one
And just across the greening field
There comes the sound of whistling steel
As trains upon their silver rails
Go sweeping past my hidden vale
Which hasn't changed in forty years
Whilst all around the Worlds in tears
A cloister hidden in the earth
Its nave this lovely - liquid church
Where quiet is found and time undone
And peace found in the spooning swans
Who gather up the main of light
Then drift beyond me - out of sight.

Ant Eater

Of fly paper his tongue is made
Of platinum his clawing spades
Cyclonic is his swinging nose
This Dyson of the termite groves.

Flotsam and Jetsam

I'm nine again - beside the sea
The bladderwrack surrounding me
For now I have a one-track mind
With X-ray specs I hope to find
A mermaid's purse - a belemnite
A dragonfly that drowned in light
A shark's tooth from the Carib sea
A clasp of Saxon jewellery
Sea glass pounded by the waves
A sabre tooth from long drowned caves
A rook lost from the Lewis Hoard
A Viking sword swept overboard
King John's treasure
Narwhal tusks
Armadas sunk in gales of rust
With - here and there
The glint of gold
An Inca's ransom in the hold…
A seagull wakes me from my trance
I gaze across the waves to France
I'm nine again - beside the sea
A small boy lost in reverie.

Lower Light

As summer opens the doors of Spain
I look to the leaves of Autumn
Mottled and blotched as a fading hand
Gently preferring the lower light
The dimmer-switch of the fading year
For this is the season I harvest most
When the World is poised between wine and Winter.

Night Thoughts of an Oak Tree: *For J.R.R. Tolkien*

I am the sarsen stag
Tossing my antlers in the wind-washed forest
I am Saint Francis - preaching to the Parliament of birds
I am circles within circles
Each year is a ring on my wooden fingers.
I am the clothes-horse for all kinds of weather
An acorn thrown into the lake of time
I provide shade for my own enlightenment
In Winter I am the pearly king
Covered as I am in buds of starlight
In Summer I wear the crown of the mistletoe vine
I am the oldest wood - in the oldest wood
Since my birth I have sheltered
Druids - Canterbury pilgrims - and Flower children
Kings have hidden in my gilded tines
Afraid only of adze and lightning
Ships - cathedrals - and the chain saw's whine
I take the long view
The years flicker by
My leaves take a sip of rain-water wine
I may put down roots here
I may put down roots
But let's not be hasty
All in good time....
All in wood time.

Horse Whisperer: *For G.K. Chesterton*

I was the ass that bucked and brayed
Before the crowds that wept and prayed

Upon my back a gentle man
Reached out his gently loving hand

He calmed me with a whispered kiss
I never knew a man like this...

The palm fronds gently paved our way
Before he left he gave me hay

And said he'd come to whisper signs
To tame all men and make them kind

Then said he'd been - in Herod's time
A stable boy from Palestine.

Tutankhamen's Candle: *Item catalogued as found*

Amongst the jumble of his reign
Most poignant was this secret flame
A simple - elemental torch
Of calcite crystal - finely wrought
Beside the treasures heaped around
The gilded thrones and peacock crowns
It seemed a gimcrack hand me down
But one night Carter - needing light
To work on objects of delight
Poured oil into its lucent cup
And as the flame began to flare
A secret picture flickered there
A lovely magic lantern slide
Of lovers in the countryside
The boy king and his sister queen
Entwined upon a floating screen
A valentine incised in stone
Much brighter than a thousand thrones
Which burnt with an eternal flame
And made the watcher feel ashamed
That - scrabbling for things so rare
He'd missed the greatest treasure there.

Note on poem: It must be said, in Carter's defence that, although the lure was - initially the glint of gold, circumstances... or the gods... ? conspired against him and he was to spend the last seven years in the tomb documenting its contents without financial recompense from the Egyptian Government who sequestered all the archaeologist's rights to the treasure and claimed the boy king as their own; although Carter's reward came in the recognition of a life of love and beauty which ended tragically and had little to do with its glittering outward trappings. Many now think, after much circumstantial and forensic evidence that Tutankhamen was murdered on the instructions of his aged vizier Ay who then conspired to marry and murder Ankhesenamen and her projected Hittite suitor, sought out in a desperate and despairing attempt to continue the royal line since her two miscarriages with Tutankhamen had left them without an heir. It is an irony of history that Ay who succeeded Tutankhamen as Pharaoh is now almost forgotten and that Tutankhamen who was despised as the heir of Akhenaten and expunged from the royal record is, as a consequence the only Pharaoh to have sailed down to us with his inventory virtually intact. He is and will remain the eternal Lord of the West - and his love for Ankhesenamen and her love for him has triumphed over anything that history or the evil deeds of men could do to quench its flame.

Rhinoceros

Durer's engraved behemoth
Descendent of Triceratops
He lurches on the dust filled plain
A quivering - horn capped mountain range
A tank with sides of dimpled iron
Impregnable to prides of lions
A fossil from another age
That rumbles down this printed page
He's Rommel in a leather coat
Binoculars around his throat
He's Goering in an armoured car
He's Churchill with a fat cigar
And yet his fate seems signed and sealed
His horn is his Achille's heel
And as he charges - turns and brakes
The Chinese measure out his fate
Ingesting powdered rhino horn
To keep their old libidos warm
And turn the Durer back to stone
By picking up a mobile phone.

After Cerebral Aneurism: *For Heather*

She wears the No mask in a play
Behind her head is cut away

A third of her no longer there
The face a mask to hide despair

They wheel her in - they wheel her out
She takes her pills - she doesn't shout

She knew me when I came to stay
But can't remember yesterday

She's Heather still - but watered down
Imprisoned in her dressing gown

Her left side useless - all at sea
The vicar came and stayed for tea

She has her faith - she bears her cross
The Lord has gained - but we have lost

Her book has torn its central spine
The pages fall out all the time

And people come and visit less
They cannot face her emptiness

It's all so sad - this grinning mask
Where Heather was - there's just the past.

The Ice Whale: *High Cup Nick, Yorkshire*

Here lies the fossil of the ice whale
Here gapes the awesome baleen mouth

Which sieved and strained the mountain out
And here lie the rocks that pocked his skin

Embedded deeply - driven in..

He calved from valleys high up there
His mother polar wind and air

Then slithered down this millstone stair

A molten - seething - fissured thing
That scoured the land he floundered in

Then vanished in the harpoon sun

A hundred thousand spuming tons
That flowered like a million guns

Then let his life blood overrun
To leave this chasm

Rainbow - hung...

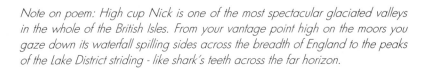

Note on poem: High cup Nick is one of the most spectacular glaciated valleys in the whole of the British Isles. From your vantage point high on the moors you gaze down its waterfall spilling sides across the breadth of England to the peaks of the Lake District striding - like shark's teeth across the far horizon.

Daddy Long Legs: *For Alison, Annie, Lucy, Sara ,Lloyd and Shelby*

A Heath Robinson contraption
A flying Citroen 2 C.V.
Icarus building an airfix model of an archangel in 60 instalments
(Most of which he never collected)
A spaced out cowboy
Scarce half made up
Not fit for purpose
All gangly legs
All dangly guy ropes
No cruise control
No automatic pilot
No one in the spindly cockpit
Breakfast left half eaten on the Marie Celeste
Just an aimless - thistledown wanderlust
A blundering asbo with two left wings
And a morbid desire to crash land in candles
DNA taking pot luck
Everything thrown to the scribbly winds
The Autumn sky full of kamikaze snowflakes
Salvador Dali twiddling his etch-a-sketch
God writing
Could do better
In the margins of creation.

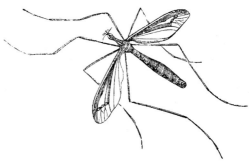

Imbolc Invocation

You came - like the first snowdrop
Out of the implacable sorrow of Winter
A votive candle in flickering darkness
A wind-washed lantern
Cradled by green-sleeve wings
A living torch from the Autumn beacon
A slow fuse
Burning in the iron earth
Snowdrop
Keeper of the flame
You are the flower of new beginnings
Epiphany's gift to the virgin earth
A swaddled rush-light in the wind and rain
Another chance come round again
To dance with love and purge the blame
To break old hatred's rusty chains
To truly love - to really change
To make our lives a sacred flame
The constellations re-arranged
A new moon over ancient lanes.

Green Man

I am the voice who sings from trees
My tongues are all unfurling leaves
I am the Greenwood's Lord of mirth
I am the mouthpiece of the earth

I am the lord of all misrule
I am the singing dancing fool
I am the lychgate in your soul
That leads you back through fields of gold

I am the seasons passing by
I am the sun who warms the sky
I am the source of all you know
The spring from which all waters flow

I am a clearing in your heart
A quiet place in an antlered park
I am your inner leaf-clad guide
I am the Green Man by your side.

And the Winner is...?

The daffodils score every time
Performance brilliant - script sublime
They are the Oscars of the Spring
And flower - just in time to win
They carry off the Garden Globes
Before a rose can blow her nose
Are found in Tatler - Cosmo - Vogue
The other flowers are just too late
Can only clap - gesticulate
They did their best - but can't compete
With such a cloud of Meryl Streep's
"Perhaps next year...?" the snowdrops say
Then hang their heads
And melt away.

Children of Albion

An ox - an ass - a manger - straw
Well this is what the children draw

And on the Lake of Galilee
Potato prints splosh out to sea

And on a hill there's Postman Pat
Who's watching Jesus with his cat

And on a cross a gold-topped man
Is crucified by Pritt-Stick hands

If we could draw what children draw
Then we would see what Jesus saw

But - growing old we rub away
The crayoned star from Christmas day.

Flea

If you could leap the Empire State
Or windsurf on a Martian sea
You would achieve - in humans terms
The prowess of the tiny flea
Who takes such measures in his stride
Whilst abseiling an elk hound's side
Or climbing up a polar bear
An Everest of frosted hair.

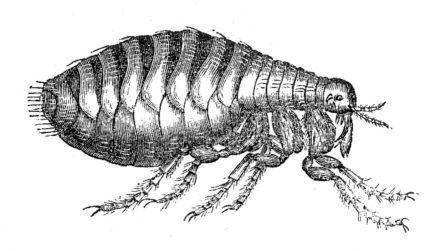

Blue Whale

The Blue Whale is the fading symbol of our failing blue Earth
The deep's great blue Buddha
The jewel in the lotus
Fashioned from fathoms of marbled blubber and sun
Our globe's vast - singing - echoing
Om Mani Padme Hum
Our Globe's numinous - paradise spouting
Umbrageous Leviathan
Forever fluke thrashing
Forever sea grazing
Swallowing spiralling galaxies of squid light
Her brain as large as a thunder cloud
Her eyes as languid as limpid meteors
With a thousand and one shades of cerulean surf
Embedded in the saga of her keel and girth
The Blue Whale is the fading symphony of our failing blue Earth
Her frame as vast as an undersea church
Her songs sea psalms to her progeny's birth
But what - in Heaven's name is she worth
This gentle - compassionate - fantastical ark
Floating down forty million years of fearless felicity?
Well - seemingly... Nothing
Till the whalers came - and the harpoon's arc
The factory ships
And the flensing dark...
And yet the Blue Whale is the failing cymbal of our failing blue Earth
And as I gingerly touch her smiling contours
In the Natural History Museum - on a rainy day
All I know is that...Here
Large is unbearably - unspeakably beautiful
Like Everest swathed in fog
And all I know is that
Here - in this one magical moment of
Awesome - childlike contemplation
All the achievements of mankind
Feel small as a mote of dust in the azure eyes of God.

Ley Lines

The silver streams run underground
Through mountain - marsh and stony town

They are sweet harp strings - softly tanned
Their warp and weft a Celtic band

And when they're struck by bardic hands
The waters run from shining sands

And when they're plucked the music hangs
The ley lines gleam throughout the land.

Elizabethan

I see you in that certain light
That gives romance its breadth and height
The way you move - the way you smile
Gives to my thoughts a single file
In which I place your treasured looks
The eyes that like an angler hooks
And plays me out upon a line
Forgetting that my flesh is thine
And would come willingly to shore
To feast upon your gaze the more
A model in my perfect scene
You have the measure of my dreams
Where I am king and you are queen
As crowns towards each other lean
As sweet peas round a bole entwine
Our souls are tangled round one vine
We fit together - hand-in-glove
Come live with me and be my love...
You do not know I wish you mine
But I would be your Valentine.

Walrus: *For Barry White - The Walrus of Love*

Skinny dipping can't describe
Balletic Bunters - sunny side
Three triple Macs - a large French fries
Washed down with baked Alaska pies
Their teeth stick out like ice pick forks
Encased in casks of Arctic pork
Their eyes are red - their hide is grey
They dine on clam-bake every day
They once inspired a fashion craze
For hirsute lips in bygone days
Ungainly on the ice and snow
They revel in the seas below
A school of airships on the move
Dirigibles with flippered screws
They fly beneath the polar waves
Great Colonel Blimps at fat boy raves
Astronauts of frigid space
Archangels of Titanic grace
Sumo wrestlers of the floes
The man - the bear their only foes
Beneath the strobe light of the sun
The Borealis leads them on
Great Barry Whites in polar bars
They groove beneath the Summer stars.

Iron Man (with flowers): *For Ted Hughes*

He minted
Mined the language brew
It felt so old
And yet so new
He made us see a pollen grain
He re-invented wind and rain
He was I guess a piece of God
A Druid with a lightning rod
And yet he was as delicate as fog
A lumberjack who rolled on logs
The man of Gnat Psalm
Eye of Crow
The dance of Kali
Carved in snow
Interrogation was his game
By moth light
Or by roaring flame
He melted iron and made a man
Then planted snowdrops in his hand
He was the children's wizard man
Who adults couldn't understand
Who climbed inside a fox's head
Slipped inside flowers and Shakespeare's bed
And seemed to know what snow flakes said
Whilst blowing past the garden shed
So now he's gone it don't seem right
Like Stonehenge stolen in the night
Yet now he's gone it don't seem wrong
He's just gone back where he belongs
Where wind is wind
And birds are birds
Whilst he's the one who just observes
That hills are made of lemon curd
And rivers run through fields of words.

Exposition of the Elephant Man
For John Merrick - A cultured and graceful human being

"Lay your sleeping head my love
The World was never good enough.."

Examine here - in grotesque form
This aberration from the norm
The bulbous head
Beneath this sack
The Lisp with which it answers back.
This monster shows how far we've risen
From lesser creatures in their prisons
This beast is something caught between
The missing - link that haunts our dreams
We should be thankful - as we gaze
That we have risen from the caves
To stand as Lords of all Creation
And pity those of lower station
Who cannot think or feel as we
Encased in brute biology.

Note on Poem: John Merrick stands as the most tragic example of that misbegotten belief that beauty is only skin deep. Indeed he stands for all those who we perceive as other, whether it be through class, creed, physical or mental disfigurement. He is the cross on which we hang all our most ill conceived and misbegotten prejudices, even more so when his nickname is taken into account - for here elephant is also used as a term of derogatory abuse for the animal kingdom as well. John Merrick is the prism through whom we see all our prejudices for what they are. The Elephant Man starring John Hurt and Anthony Hopkins is a masterpiece and one of the most moving films I have ever seen.
To add further insult to injury his actual name was Joseph, not John. Dr Frederick Treves ascribed the name John to him when writing one of his case reports and this is the name by which he is commonly known.

Musk Oxen: *For Barry Lopez*

If Jason had sailed North
He would have found the Golden Fleece
Of the Musk Oxen
Ancient cousins of the Grecian kind
As much a product of this land
As the land itself...
The breathing embodiment
As at home here as we are
Curled up with the Sunday Papers
And he would have marvelled
At their sagacity
Their two million year interrogation
Of the wind
Their made to measure movements
Their diet of fire weed and willow
Darkness and light
And he would have wished
That he too
Could cease his wanderings
Drop anchor in the pack ice
And learn something about
Patience - endurance...
And the healing to be had
From these hoary Buddha's
Wrapped in snow flakes
Drifting under the Bo Tree
Of the North Star.

Chaucer's Bluebells: *The Nuns of Walsingham, North Norfolk*

A blue tide floods the Green Man's wood
A sward of nuns with lapis hoods
Hail Mary's swaying to and fro
On pilgrimage the maidens go
To see their master drop his head
And hips turn all the hedgerows red
To see their Saviour conquer death
And rise again as living bread
To see their Lord once more take breath
Infuse the earth with sacredness
To see the Word once more made flesh
And give this globe its bright redress.

26

Sutton Hoo Helmet

Who gazed through these moonless eyes
And lay within this ghostly ship...?
For thirteen hundred acid years
The thief of time devoured his gifts
Yet even time could not dissolve
The timeless glint of timeless gold
The bird that framed these moonless eyes
That gazed out over storm-lit skies
His soul flew briefly through the hall
Then arced through windows dark and tall
He flew into the Pagan night...
Or did he find the light of Christ...?
He lies between these drifting lands
A shifting soul on shifting sands
A Janus looking back and forth
From Christian South to Viking North
To Valhalla or Avalon
To which one has the storm cock gone...?
A weather-vane upon a hill
His spirit drifts about here still.

Note on poem: The defining feature of the Sutton Hoo Helmet is the gilded bird that delineates the moonless face of the ancient warrior. The owner of the helmet is thought - on good authority to be Raedwald, one of a line of Saxon Kings who ruled East Anglia at this time. The complex of Sutton Hoo is seen by many as a Pagan redoubt surrounded by a Christian sea, but the tide was turning and certain kings in Sweden, who were buried in ship mounds were later re-interred by their recently converted sons in newly built churches hard by the promontories of the old religion. The Sutton Hoo helmet is associated - in the popular imagination with Beowulf the hero figure of the poem of the same name which lies, like a great Viking burial mound filled with a glittering word hoard at the very beginning of English Literature. The poem was written sometime in the eighth century (around the time that the complex of Sutton Hoo was being created) by an anonymous Christian monk and although the poem harks back to an earlier period in Scandinavian history there were strong links between the Danish and Anglo-Saxon cultures and - for many the Sutton Hoo Helmet is the helmet of the mythic hero who defeated Grendel.

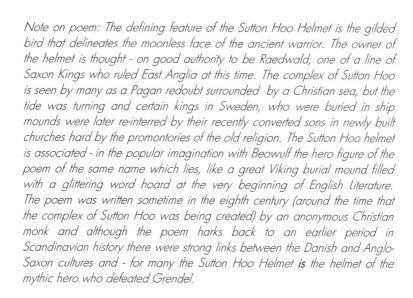

Angler Fish

A deep sea dong
With a luminous nose
More surreal than Lear could compose
The angler fish has its own porch light
To welcome guests in the dead of night
The light says there's bed and board to be had
But the teeth say there's nothing but the butcher's slab
As this comely moll with the alluring fag
Cruises like a bacon-slicer dressed in drag.

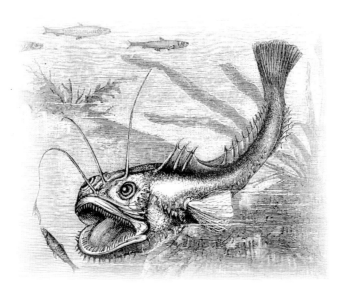

Ratty: *For Kenneth Grahame*

The Wind in the Willows reveals the form
Of a water rat at The Gates of Dawn

On the banks of Toad's expansive hall
Where the ducks are a - dabbling up tails all

We find a hamper made of reeds
With potted shrimps and stilton cheese

Comestibles of every kind
For a Cambridge blue with a first-class mind

Upon a willow pattern plate
Beneath the weir - beside the lake

The water rat take tea and cake
And reads the works of William Blake

He's English as the day is long
He hums the Eton boating song

And lies beside Old Father Thames
Through afternoons that never end

Just out of reach - just round the bend
The Mole's enchanting whiskered friend.

The Green Man's Book of Days

January
The Poet and the Blackbird

My gold-nibbed pen
And this famished blackbird
Both scratching a living
On Winter's empty page.

February
Snowdrops

Dutch girls
Laughing
In the Winter market.

March
Kate Moss and other Narcissi

Leggy models on Spring's catwalk
Daffodils sway their willowy hips
And pout their luscious lemony lips
Then turn their heads towards the sun
The paparazzi's flashing guns.

April

Easter Sunday
The scarecrow missing
From the moonlit field.

May
Postcard from North Norfolk

Crab farmer smoking
On the rusty tractor
Smock as faded
As the springtime sky.

June

Cornflowers winking
Like the eyes of Vikings
Battle weary in Summer fields.

July
Bicycling to Happisburgh

Lighthouse painted by a child
Sellotaped
To the blue horizon.

October
Autumn on Beacon Hill

The moon
Glimpsed
Through the birch's negligee.

August
Tommy Cooper - Incognito

Feeling sorry for the sunburnt scarecrow
I gave him a fez
Some clouded Ray-bans.

November

On the fields of the Somme
Perennially bleeding
A red mist...hovers...

September
Contraceptive Moon

As she takes her pills
So the moon glides slowly
Round the silver packet.

December
Winter Goldfish

Under the ice the goldfish glow
Like Christmas clementines
Wrapped in snow.

Great Expectations

First love is a kind of youthful madness
A March Hare feeling of lamb-springing gladness
Which - seen down the telescope of swirling years
Is nothing but a foretaste of madeleine tears
The smiles all now perceived as fake
The weevils in the wedding cake
The hands on time's enchanted face
Now rusting in the unwound case
And all the joys you once expected
Ephemeral as Blake's directive.

Swallow: *For Jeannie, John and Pauline*

Blue-toothed barnstormer
Surfing the internet of Earth
Hard drive - hot wired for the Haj
Star sailor - dune skimmer
Spitfire pilot with a Satnav badge
A bird of brilliant lapis hue
A hieroglyph of morning dew
Following the caravanserai
Inculcated with the genome of instinctive pilgrimage
Twisting with the Autumn leaves
From his mud hut under the tithe barn eaves
Obeying the planet's turning face
The master key of his migrating race
A heavenly - winging - apostate splinter
A bridegroom fleeing the Snow Queen of Winter
Nothing has prepared him for his journey
From Cape Wrath to the Cape of Good Hope
From lychgates freckled with fading confetti
To the teeming plains of the Serengeti
But he is pilot from the egg
Already scrambled in his very being
He has all the notes of the rally driver
In the glove compartment of his heart
All the charts are inscribed
In the wheel house of his soul
His blazing path is strong and true
From Tavistock to Timbuktu
From seas of green to seas of blue
Sextant - astrolabe - compass rose
As Autumn comes - the swallow goes
He sets his jib - the wild winds blow
And toss the flibbertigibbet to and fro
A fair weather friend
In the clotted cream skies
Of Anglican Devon
He trusts his storm driven
Southward spinning journey
His African safari
To the Benin bronzed witch doctor
Of Ouija board Heaven.

33

The Passing of the Buffalo

The buffalo are melting ice bison
Fog wildebeest
Once they swarmed on the western plains
Like deafening shag pile
Once Indians made a culture and a civilization from their
Tidal beauty
They clothed themselves in thunder
They fished with thunder
They carried their children in thunder cribs
They made love under heaving thunder leather
They painted these coal gods on their shamanic breasts
They decorated their lives with their reason for living
But then the White Man came
And shot the buffalo from trains
To process them into meaninglessness.
And the buffalo left the plains like weeping smoke
And there was no more thunder
And there was no more love making
And there were no more children

And there was no reason for living.

The Globe: *For Sam Wanamaker*

The thatching glows like bearded gold
The structure heaves - and in its hold
The musings of a flickering man
Will burn across the watching land
As Shakespeare rises from his sleep
The World contained inside his keep
The characters inside his head
Are wakened from their vellum beds
Bardolph - Pistol - Shallow - all
They flock towards the prompter's call
The ghost of Burbage bows his head
And Will Kemp jigs on donkey's legs
Leontes eyes his glass of wine
And Macbeth mouths the dagger lines
As players camp beside their fires
The playwright moves between the pyres
To test the waters of his thought
Disguised as one his muse brought forth..
The cloak of tongues has spread the word
And leavened up the common herd
The flag proclaims the play on view
And destiny awaits its cue...
The Folio is open now
And Ariel takes the nuptial bow
A wind fills out the swelling scene
The Globe returns from history's dream.

Worzel Gummidge gets Personal

Feeling sorry for the lonely scarecrow
I put an ad in the personals

Out-door type would like to meet corn dolly
For bird watching
Must enjoy country pursuits…

Field and grid reference supplied

Previous Aunt Sallies need not apply…

(No time wasters… football rattles… or bin liners)

Heron

I am rod
And I am line
A switchblade knife
That
Given time
Will turn this water into wine
For Nature carved me from the air
To be the bird that isn't there
Yet through the looking-glass I spy
The apple of my gimlet eye
I slash down from my mist-wrapped hide
The mirror cracks from side to side
I fly between the dusk and dawn
Leave moonlit scales upon the lawn.

Astrologers

We need them more than they need us
The three kings
Gold-leaf blowing in the desert wind
Only in Matthew do they ride across the page
But - from these dusty verses we have tapped
An oasis of invention
With their gifts of gold - frankincense and myrrh
They glide on by
For all of us need to be announced
All of us need to feel gifted
All of us need to feel lifted
All prefigured in some eternal sky.

Factory Farmed

The salmon farmer
Has impounded the constellations
Furled the sails of Magellan
Locked up the waterfalls
Switched off the moon
Turned the salmon's poetry
Into Gradgrind's fact filled prose...
This battery farm of the water
Has sucked all the hazel wisdom from the Druid's fish
To give us his flesh on a Habitat dish
The call of the wild fills the salmon's soul
But the stars shine down on his festering shoal
A donkey of water
He turns the wheel
Whilst the lice burrow into his pointless keel.

39

John Clare's January

A carillon of silent bells
Is pealing in the Winter wood
The Green Man lights the aconites
That flare beneath their snowdrop hoods
The children make a man of snow
Hang round his neck a holly bow
The robin searches for a worm
Wherever Winter clods are turned
And Jack the postman blows his nail
Delivering the Winter mail.
The squirrel in his Winter dray
Is dreaming of the nuts of May
The dormouse in his ball of hay
Is snuffling through a Summer's day
The kingfisher in rainbow plume
Now hurtles through the frosty gloom
And in the fusty otter holt
The kits all hear the rusty bolts
Of ice now creaking in the race
Beneath the mill-wheel's moonlit face.

Gorillas or Guerrillas…?

Once upon a myth
When I was much younger
And much less hirsute than I am now
I finally came face to knee-cap
With the ghastly gorilla in my local museum..
Now I'd seen specimens of him in the local pub
He was a skyscraper of moth eaten savagery
An equatorial troll
Wildly brandishing a brain smashing club
Killed - in the nick of time
By a *noble* Victorian hunter
Of *unquestionably* bluer evolutionary blood
For a long time after this I thought that
Gorillas were Guerrillas
For a long time after this I thought that Fidel Castro
Was a wild - cigar puffing ape
Who used Malibu aftershave
And ruled a place called Cuba
With an iron banana in a velvet glove
It was only later I realized that Gorillas were **not** Guerrillas
It was only after David Attenborough I realized that
After dying of gout in the Gentleman's Club
It was the *noble* Victorian hunter who should have been
STUFFED
And mothballed in the museum of mankind's savage ways
To teach errant Gorilla school children
A salutary lesson
On rainy days…….

"*We know very little of their daily lives, for they are seldom seen except by those who hunt them, and who have but little chance of watching their habits. But all that we do know teaches us that that in their rough way they have developed into strangely man - like though savage creatures, while at the same time they are so brutal and so limited in their intelligence that we cannot but look upon them as degenerate animals, equal neither in beauty, strength, discernment, nor in any of the nobler qualities, to the faithful dog, the courageous lion, or the half-reasoning elephant.*"
Arabella Buckley, author of Winners in Life's Race.
The standard text book for well heeled Victorian school children…!

Winter Mourner
Earlham Road Cemetery, Norwich

She paused by the rose
Began to pray
A human candle
On a Winter's day
I watched her from a bench nearby
The rose
The girl
The light
And I
We were both framed by something vast
The flags all frozen at half mast
But then the flags unfurled at last
A grief observed
The angels passed…

Otters: *For Virginia McKenna and Gavin Maxwell*

Bright eyed mermammals
Slick backed and sharp suited
Wearing the water like a second skin
Otters disport their barnstorming beauty
Displacing their torsos with web-fingered wings
Twisting themselves like gymnast's ribbons
In arabesques of refracted light
Otters elope through their aqueous kingdom
Like sinuous smoke rings from Poseidon's pipe
Like head-scarves
Cascading from soft-tops in flight
Gawky above but God like below
They glide between worlds like a svelte shadow show
Dissolving in light like a lithe swirling brush
Like the scent of Chanel on a Jaguar's plush
Dissolving in time like a shy Geisha's blush
Like the Cheshire Cat's grin
On a loch's midnight hush.

Bob Hope's Camel

Martian hooves - a hairy hump
A wild - odiferous fly-whisked rump
The Ancient World is her spittoon
Her breath would make an old skunk swoon
Her teeth were nicked from King Tut's mother
Her lips are made of indiarubber...
Her song is like the muezzin's call
As from the minaret he falls
Her manners are uncouth and slow
Her legs are knock-kneed down below
And yet her eyes are liquid gold
The desert's pouting centrefold
And - in a mirage she may seem
Like Mrs Lamour in a dream
To dance around your caravan
Whilst on the road to Samarkand.

Do not go Gently

The polar bear
Is treading on thin ice
Walking on frosty eggshells
Waiting for his frozen savannah
To crystallize
Out of nothing
For the moment he is in purgatory
He has a passport
But no country
A borderline case
Perfected for a non-existent landscape
He scavenges on the edge of his ghostly dominion
Which is melting beyond his reach
A down and out on skid row
He lumbers amongst the trash cans
A frosty Grendel on the edge of sight
He blunders outside the oil fired mead hall of humanity
Under the pipelines of black gold
He rages - dirty woolly bear white
A species at the end of its tether
He rages under the borealis
RAGES - RAGES - RAGES
Against the dying of the ice.

Bee Orchids: *For Sara*

Pouting on Nature's street corners
Orchids are salacious
Evolved to brightly please
Mutton dressed as lamb
They are hookers dressed as bees
Honey-pots for nectar louts
Who go down on their knees
To cross their palms with pollen
And ensure that orchids breed.

46

Yeti

Red haired
Splay-footed
Sasquatch of the snow fields
Sometimes glimpsed amongst the frangipani
He lumbers on the edge of our imagination
Our shy snow cousin
So shy he barely exists
This gentle shepherd of snowdrifts
And herder of yaks
Is he watching us behind our backs…?
Is he merely cut-price Zen
A Koan for Western mountaineering men …?
Then again
Is he perhaps like the snow leopard…?
Can he drift invisibly amongst the prayer flagged stupas
Like a Guru from the springs of the Brahmaputra
Or is he always the lurching sky loner
Pummelling the thunder clouds of his chest
Breasting avalanches in his shaggy vest
Wreathed in incense and Buddhist charms
Ordering the weather with his Herculean arms…?
Well - the truth is
No one really knows
For no one has ever caught a Yeti
Brian Blessed mooning on a cross channel ferry
Or even brought one down with verbal confetti
But - before I go
And before he comes to guide you
From the Tibetan Book of the Dead
Try to picture him
Cloaked in red
The World's oddest - most elusive scene stealer
Reflecting the Himalayan sunrise
In his Ray-bans of frosted silver.

Jane Austen sums it up…

I thought you were what you were not
And thinking so has fouled my lot

Not just with you - but others who
Thought I was what they wanted too

They did not see me through my smile
Or else they would have run a mile

The problem lies with who we seem
To others living in a dream

Of what they take a mate to be
Beneath a physiognomy

If characters were portrayed out
There'd be less marriages about

And plainer Jane's would surely find
That men would flock as Valentines

To those who bear a finer grace
Beneath a sad and careworn face.

Hare

The hare is the quivering high command
Of hare intelligence
Feeling the wind with his Fylingdale whiskers
Turning his hare-brained velvet radar
His whole early warning system of hare
Into the twitching landscape
Listening
For the thoughts of foxes
The dreams of eagles
Transfixed in a cats-cradle
Of his own cross-eyed uncertainty
A Jack-in-the box
Waiting to leap
To all points of the compass
A paranoid schizophrenic
Sectioned by his own senses
A harp of hare
Mad as March
Shaking on the edge of his daft horizon
Quaking in the shadow of his own reflection.

Foggy Morning above Lathkildale: *For Ted Hughes*

Out of the ewe's rear end
Hangs the afterbirth of an Apollo mission
The lamb
Parachuted from the dark side of the moon
Trailing the bloodied ripcords
And the pearly placenta
The whole sun blessed cargo
The glistening evisceration
Licked into bleating shape
By the baaing Mother ship
Anchored on the soft green swell of Derbyshire.

A Poem for a.w. *(Wainwright)*

He captured landscape - line by line
By cross-hatching he helped define
The mountains for an armchair mind
With nothing but a pen and scrapers
He put the mountains down on paper
Within his bending compass came
The daffodils - the tarns - the lanes
The Lakes - the vistas - frame by frame
Within his books there are contained
Like convolutions of the brain
The routes up every mountain range
The loveliness is all arranged
The paths made clear - the cairns maintained
And in a time of ceaseless change
His books endure - the fells remain
As signposts to a world more sane
Where Nature's Queen in glory reigns
Where rainbows arch through mist and rain
Where man no longer feels estranged
From everything the Lord once named
Where Eden's past can be reclaimed
And poets walk in God's domain.

Seals..?: *In memory of Kathleen and for her daughter Tricia*

Michelin mermaids
In tarpaulin slacks

Neptunian call-girls
Entrancingly fat

Sirens who slip
Between ocean and air

Then ooze onto beaches
To fuss with their hair

Divas who lurch
Between ocean and sand

Then cruise down to Cannes
To get cellulite tanned.

Song of the Year's Turning

I listen to the song of the year's turning
The geese
Creaking towards the North Star
The dormouse
Weaving her Winter womb
The anthem of leaf fall
The absence of Evensong
The tide of remembrance
Rising and falling
The wind
Plucking the harp of the rowan
The scarecrow busking for a hatful of moonshine.

If you go Looking...

If you go looking for daffodils
Search for the wild ones
Not the gilded battledores of the garden centre
The armies of Xeroxed halberdiers
But Wordsworth's curtseying Lenten lilies
The dancing maids of Buttermere.

Road kill: *For Ted Hughes*

I found her in the tangled grass by the cemetery wall
As if laid out by someone ashamed
Tarnished - inadvertently with the mark of Cain
There was a kind of awkward reverence here
A furtive kind attempt at ceremony
As if some forlorn suburban shaman
Had tried to make peace with her gypsy spirit
I glanced - voyeuristically embarrassed - at her rosy nipples
And the fading warmth of her body
Stiffening amongst the daffodils
And I wondered if...
Perhaps her cubs were still waiting for their treasured mother
The russet smile at the foxy hole
And the dangling promise of her milky stole
And I pondered...
How many of us ever stop to think - as Larkin did
Of the hedgehog and the mower...?
The repercussions that ripple out across the universe
When some fox cubs lose their mother
Or we didn't say I'm sorry
Before death reclaimed that lover
How many of us ever stop to think
What a vixen's life is worth
As she makes her dreamtime journeys
On the song lines of the earth...?
How many of us ever stop and stare
And wish that life was moving on the verge of our despair
That love could find the latchkey to the prison of our lair
Rewind us to the moment that is gone beyond repair
Where the fox runs wild and tame less past the car that is not there
Where the driver now is blame less
And the Fates were not unfair
Where the one who was our lover
Was assured we always cared
That the sadness they occasioned
Was a moment's maudlin flare
Which was long ago absolved into the moments that we shared
Where the cubs can taste their mother
Smell the foxgloves in her hair
And the milk of human kindness
Fills the pregnant evening air.

Persephone's Daughter

Now - on the tide - as Winter turns
The spectrum of the World returns
While all outside is drab and wet
The child gets our her crayon set
And - as her dreams of flowers takes flight
She colours in an aconite
Then sleep-walks over snow-swept field
The snowdrops blooming at her heels.

Star Maker: Tutankhamen's Lullaby

Each verse chanted on consecutive nights
by the priests of the chamber before
sealing the tomb.

Night 1

Now sleep - for great Anubis
Who is death's right hand
Has steered your ship of heaven
Through our gates of sand
Then pray - for your mother who is blessed
Has pressed
The seed of great Osiris
In time's swaddling bands.

Night 2

Now dream - for creeping twilight
On the cooling sands
Has rowed the groom of heaven
Into moon-kissed lands
Then sing - for your father in the West
Has blessed
The fruit of mother Isis
With his timeless hand.

Night 3

Now wake - for great Osisris
Cooled by peacock fans
Has lit this spark of Heaven
With a flaming brand
Then dance - for our Pharaoh who is Lord
Has moored
The soul of Tutankhamen
In his starlit land.

Take care.. Zebras Crossing...!

Be careful crossing the asphalt hide
Look both ways
For the lion is coming
The rush hour road
Is choked with wild eyed wildebeest

They have squashed many Zebras
Rolled them flat to make these crossings
So tread carefully on the skin of Africa

Look both ways
Before you step into the seething savannah

Stand by the imposing Belisha giraffes
Wait for the lollipop gazelle with her sun on a pole
Follow the Rift Valley Code

If necessary seek the help of the tall Masai policeman
With his uniform of ebony
And his pocket watch of western wealth

Be savannah certain
Look both ways
Be marvellously - patiently prudent
Till the lion has passed in stealth

Or you may be - unwittingly

FLATTENED

By Zebras crossing yourself...!

Harp Broken

Hush now -
Don't be afraid
For I've covered you
With the Golden Fleece
And am gently gluing you back together
Re-stringing your broken heart
To make you a lovely instrument
And a channel for my peace.

Scarecrow's Almanack

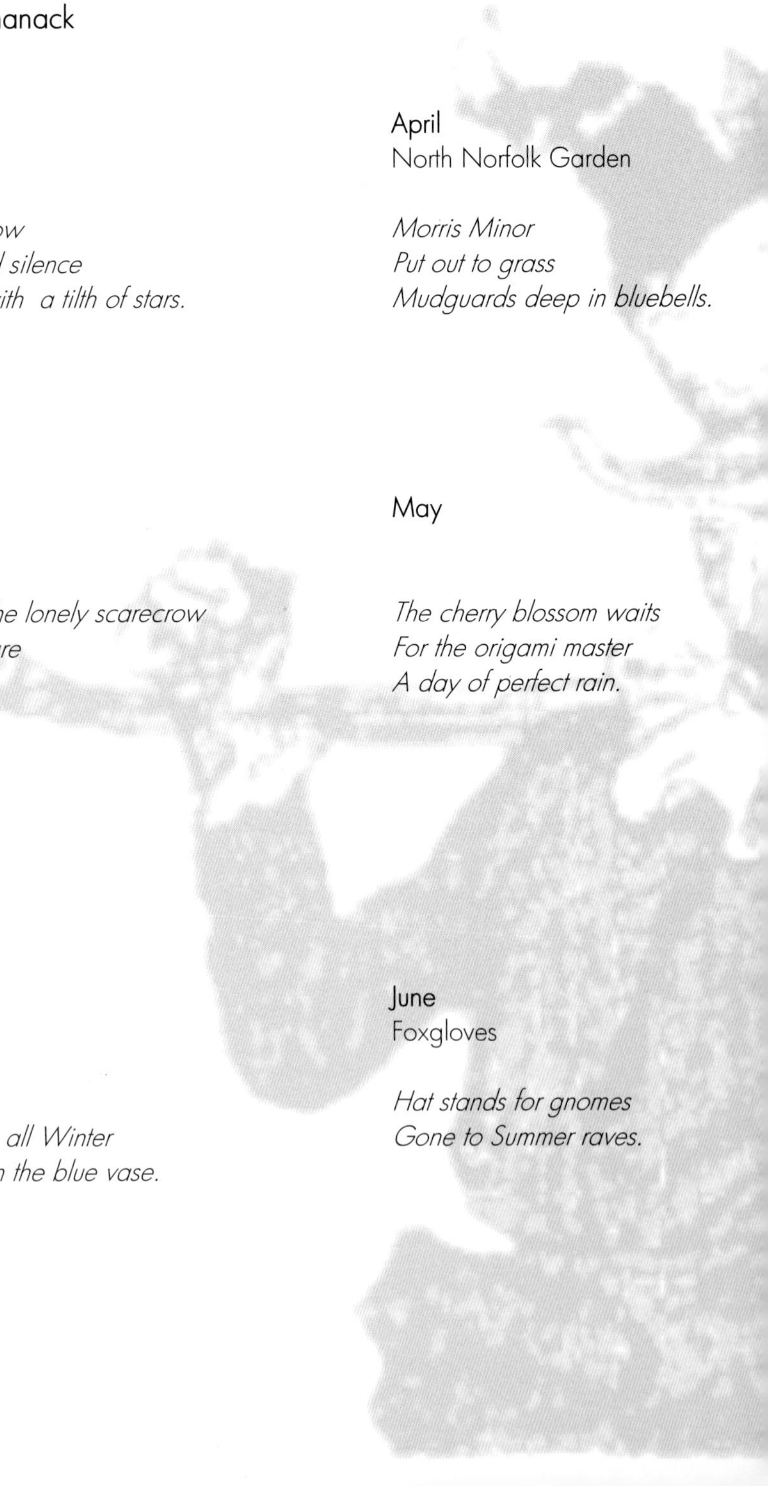

January
Sacred Snow

Outside my window
Flakes of six sided silence
Cover the earth with a tilth of stars.

February

Feeling sorry for the lonely scarecrow
I gave him a picture
Of Judy Garland.

March

This blue door
Has been waiting all Winter
For the daffodils in the blue vase.

April
North Norfolk Garden

Morris Minor
Put out to grass
Mudguards deep in bluebells.

May

The cherry blossom waits
For the origami master
A day of perfect rain.

June
Foxgloves

Hat stands for gnomes
Gone to Summer raves.

July
Hot Couture…!

The scarecrow
Wearing her Winter collection
Perspiring in the Summer field.

August
Crowd Pleaser

The pigeon might seem to be a simpleton
But every year he manages to court centre stage
At Lords - Trent Bridge and Wimbledon.

September

Our bonsai bird
The moonlit wren
This haiku flying from my pen.

October

Last night he came
The wind Grendel
And took even the little leaves
That slept beneath my hall of clouds.

November

With this sparkler
I am God as Jackson Pollock
Dripping his gilded signature
In the corner of the universe.

December
Last Post at Maes Howe

Sun posts a Christmas card
Through Orkney's Winter door
Where ox and ass and ancestors
Lie jumbled on the floor.

The Lullaby of Aengus mac Og: *The Irish God of love*

I saw you when you were not there
I heard you on a silent stair

I kissed you at a country fair
At Sligo and at County Clare

I am the stallion - you the mare
I braid the stars around your hair

I place my armour in your care
And hope in gladness you'll repair

To offer dreams we both can share
And build a home in Innisfare

Above the rocks where eagles dare
And children's laughter fills the air.

Electraglide in blue and green

Kingfisher: Newton Harcourt, Leicestershire
Late November 2006
For Pollyanna Pickering, Anna - Louise, Dad and Beryl

I caught him on the edge of sight
In Autumn's lovely lower light
A match
Struck
With a turquoise flame
Then quenched - then lit
Then quenched again
Through Autumn's sunlit Saxon hall
He hurtled like a fireball
Eloping through the waning light
A needle darning day and night
Through myrtle - snow and candlelight
A seraphim of second sight
Through mistletoe and frost and ice
The Fisher King in brush-stroked flight.

Chameleon

The chameleon
Has more colour channels than cable TV
A brilliant interference in the tropical trees
It changes hue in the blink of an eye
From BBC 1 to boxing on Sky
It moves more slowly than a cheque in the post
But its swivelling sockets are its proudest boast
Revolving independent through the arc of degrees
Like Jodrell bank on L.S.D.
As it swings around in the prehensile trees
Till the sockets engage on a plumptious moth
Which its tongue envelops in a spume of froth
Telescoping back into its horny head
End of transmission
And time for bed.

Elgar's England

Our land is crossed by old stone walls
By hedges brushed by summer squalls
Our land is crossed by ancient tracks
By ley lines rubbed from ancient maps
Our land is stitched on history's baize
A Psalter of forgotten ways
A quilt of all that's gone before
A page from Nimrod's wind blown score.

Torch Song

The sadness of the years gone by
Sends clouds across my bluebell eyes
For those I hurt I hold a flame
That sadness will not come again
For those who hurt me I forgive
For vengeance poisons how we live
We hurt as we are hurt in turn
But - gradually we start to learn
That - though our loving may be spurned
All broken hearts can be returned
Eventually the wheel will turn
And new relationships will burn
Unfurling like two angel ferns
To banish all our sad concerns.

Pheasant: *For Laurie Lee and in memory of Bernard O'Brien*

The pheasant
Is the burning flower of Autumn
The torch of Samhain
The cup bearer of the graal of Winter
Before it alighted from the damask East
The season had no emblem
The Autumn had no priest
Who could say where Autumn could be found
Until the pheasant made its entrance
On the old years burning ground...?
"I am" said the pheasant
"The winging reliquary
Samuel Palmer's golden bird
That overshadows all the world
Amalgam of the season's soul
I am the symbol of the whole
The leaves all find their end in me
I bless them with the third degree
I am the incense swinging flame
The Paschal candle in the rain
I stand for all the turning leaves
That fall from all the weeping trees
I am the bird all stitched from flame
That carries Christmas in its train
I sweep the old years threshing floor
The chaff blown through the Autumn door
I rise above the burning globe
In all my flaming harvest robes
An Inca priest upon the lawn
I strut across the Golden Dawn
The beaters flush me from the heather
In Autumn's lovely golden weather
Then blast me from the Autumn sky
A firework crashing down to die
A treasure trove of gilded swag
All stuffed into the gillies bag
Outside the poultry shop I glint
The Midas bird by Gustav Klimt."

Skunk Chanel: *For Ogden Nash*

The skunk's so famous for its stink
Wild essence of a well blocked sink
Its charming perfume made me think
Of bottling it for girls from Rome
Who'd spend long evenings on their own.

Guide Dog

A man's golden eyes
Doors of perception on all fours
Love in harness
The Labrador leads her master
Through invisible cities
She waits
With the patience of Job
By rush hour roads
Leads her master through the Red Sea
Of impatient steel
Curled at his heel
She is his sign and seal
A symbiosis through patient osmosis
The Ariadne who guides him through
The sound filled tunnels
Of a sunless world.

Queen of Candlemass

The bells of silence gently dream
All nodding by the village stream
They shine out - like a silken pleat
From Winter's snowy winding sheet
A band of ermine tinged with green
On Imbolc's lovely virgin queen
Who - pregnant with the springtime flowers
Is dancing in a Book of Hours
And holding in her milk white hands
A palantir of gilded towers
The distant battlements of Spring
From which the jocund bluebells ring.

Reindeer

The Reindeer are listening with their coat-hanger heads
To Radio Chernobyl
They have picked up something
Smelt the rotting atoms in the wind
And the Lapps are watching the Reindeer...
Kneeling in their Reindeer coats
They explore the look of puzzlement
The genuine fear of invisible invasion
The Red Army of radiation
Which is seeping into their Christmas culture
No - Father Christmas will not be flying this year
For the Reindeer are mutating
In Reindeer wombs throughout the land
Reindeer are being born
Without the power of flight
On Christmas Eve they will be waiting in their hospital beds
But their pillows will not be filled
And their hair will continue to fall like snow
And the Reindeer will continue not to come
And there will be no presents
And there will be no laughter
And the snow will fall like a cloud of skulls
Mothers will leave out sherry and mince pies
Vodka - snow cakes and warm hay
But their children's hair will continue to fall like snow
And there will be no presents
And there will be no laughter
And the snow will fall like a cloud of skulls
And the reindeer will continue not to come.

Horseshoe Crabs: *For David Attenborough*

On the strangest night of the year
When the moon is full as a crab in love
They swarm the unspoken beach

This is D-Day for the grey dinner plates

Seething in the ocean like a soup of armour
The moon trilobites
Emerge from our Cambrian nightmares
And let down their fossilized hair
For a night of frying pan love

On the strangest night of the year
When the moon is as full as a crab in love
The Horseshoe Crabs remember
That there must be *more* Horseshoe Crabs
Then the moon unlocks their stone libidos
And they clankingly embrace
Beneath the crab above
Massing like drunken Daleks
To spoon with their dustbin lid loves.

The Turin Shroud

Is this - imprinted on a shroud
The man who drew such thronging crowds
The crucified who cried aloud
Then climbed a stairway through the clouds...?
Is this emblazoned on a cloth
The King who hung upon the cross
But left behind this whip-lashed slide
Golgotha's grainy regicide
The Crown of Thorns
The blood-splashed side
A Polaroid for Eastertide...?

Note on Poem: Controversy has dogged the Turin Shroud for centuries, with many proclaiming it the genuine article, whilst others have decreed that it is just one of a gallimaufry of fakes that existed across the mediaeval Christian world with every church worthy of note having its piece of the one true cross, the sword, Spear of Destiny that speared Christ's side or The Holy Grail which was the cup containing the blood of Christ present at the last supper - or the womb of Mary Magdalene; this being one of the later heresies recently popularized by Dan Brown in his best seller The Da Vinci Code.

In recent years the shroud has been subject to scientific scrutiny by a raft of experts who proclaimed it, after carbon dating to be a mediaeval fake, albeit a very clever one, perhaps created by Leonardo Da Vinci, the face being the first experimental photograph of the Renaissance genius, however subsequent analysis has now cast doubt on the scientists' proclamations and it remains an enigma wrapped in an enigma. My own personal view is that the shroud could be the genuine article and may be the image of Christ seared onto the cloth after what Tibetan Buddhists have called a Rainbow Resurrection. Lama Govinda in his book The Way of the White Clouds describes the process in which enlightened Buddhist masters can sometimes disappear in a cloud of spectral radiation.

The best book on the subject for those wishing to pursuer the matter further is Colin Wilson's 'The Blood and the Shroud' which constructs a convincing time line for its passage through history.

Cheetah

Her pistons bathed in gracile oil
Her watch-spring movements tightly coiled
She waits for morning on the veldt
Stilettos sheathed in tensile stealth
The tears fall darkly from her eyes
The lithe gazelle beyond her lies
The bait is set - the trap is sprung
She flares from morning's smoking gun
She springs - she bites - the neck is wrung
Her cubs enjoy her tender tongue.

Oak and Rowan: *A Song*

Once we bent together like a hedge
Woven by time and weather
Once we were tenderly grafted
An Oaken man and a Rowan wife
Married together by the hedge-maker's knife
And though we are no longer spliced
Although she leads a separate life
Shadowy branches like severed limbs
Twine us across the tangled years
And when she bends I feel her stir
For I felt complete inside of her
And when she writes I know she cares
For we're joined by ghosts - by rambling tares
And though she's now a separate tree
She felt complete inside of me
And though the hedge was torn apart
She left her roots inside my heart
And when I see a Rowan tree
I feel her bend inside of me
And when she sees an Oak in leaf
My roots entwine around her feet.

Ankhesenamen's Garland

She has just left sweet Amen's room
Her perfume wafts around the tomb

Dropped at the door a last bouquet
And then the girl bride slipped away

And though three thousand years have flown
Her garland sweeps us to the throne

Where love that's life's immortal wine
Gives light to help Osiris shine

Where love that's half as old as time
Spreads wings around a golden shrine.

September 11th 2001

First Strike: North Tower

A silver otter
Diving seamlessly
Into a sea of mirrors.

Second Strike: South Tower

The plane
Crashes through my brain
On an endless loop
Lucifer torching a deck of cards
And a terrible beauty is born
Miltonian pinions of Satan
Billowing
From a grey vase.

Two Horsemen of the Apocalypse

On a bright Autumn morning
Two quicksilver bombs
The grace of a diver
The arc of a swan
On a bright Autumn morning
Two quicksilver bombs
And Yggdrasil shaking
As Ragnarok comes.

Fireman's Son: New York, September 11th

A child
Waiting on the drive
Smoke in the distance...

September 12th

The morning after
Our ASDA news stand
A wall of flame.

His last message on her answer phone
She plays it
Over and over...

On Radio 4
That grief-stricken stockbroker
Grappling with the piece of human lives.

Tonka Toy: Memorial Gardens
US Embassy London, Mid September

Everything depends
On a red fire engine
In the rain.

Icons of grief
Prayer flag photographs
Flutter down Broadway.

Argonaut: *For Kahil Gibran, Sara, Lloyd, Shelby and Ryan*

Floating in the heart-lit flood
In the ovoid loom of the womb
Love is weaving an ark of life
A coracle of tiny bones
A vestige from an ancient sea
A brilliant scrap of destiny
Entwined around a fleur-de-lys
A brain that's made of flowers and light
A spine that's carved from anthracite
A rib cage that contains the air
A skull that's fleeced with seaweed hair
And through those eyes - the doors of time
A creature looks - not yours - not mine
But something other shuffling through
A Moses in a caul of blue
A sailor made with gentle glue
A stowaway that time re-drew
Keelhauled upon the wheel of strife
Another being crying "life"
Press-ganged to join the Gaian crew
This Argonaut from me to you.

Red Squirrel Memory: *For Mary Mclean*

I cup the leaf flame in my head
I hoard the haw light roaring red
And let it warm my Autumn bed
Through Winter storms I'm lantern led.

Red Squirrel

You glimpse him
As a hill top on fire
Elizabeth's chestnut hair
A blink of burning memory
Cordite - tinder-box and musket
The Iron Age stain of hilltop towns
Now fading from our country's crown
The russet ink from Shakespeare's pen
That bound us as a race of men
You glimpse him as the chestnut thread
That tied the May Pole round our heads
The broad-leaved woodland's natural heir
Who scampered round the Green Man's chair
But now the woodland's lost its light
The Dryad has been put to flight
And where the jewel of Autumn flared
The Crown of England's dark and bare.

John Cooper Clarke's Giant Squid Rap

*Or Daphne entertains Scylla and Charybdis
(A Poem Tennyson might have written...
if he hadn't thought better of it)*

I'm eighty feet from beak to sucker
Tea clippers are my bread and butter

At twenty thousand leagues I glide
With tentacles that suck and writhe

At twenty thousand leagues I hide
Then lash the sperm whale's oily side

My angler fish are chandeliers
That light my boudoir's nameless fears

And here I spread a feast for friends
Of Danish pastries filled with men

I am the Kraken of the deep
The reason sailors seldom sleep

I'm eighty feet full fathom five
With dinner plates for Wedgwood eyes

At twenty thousand feet I thrive
Godzilla's underwater bride

From twenty thousand leagues I rise
Medusa on the evening tide.

Santa Claus visits Earlham Road Cemetery, Norwich

For Jack and Robert Frost

The graveyard here is cold and bleak
But children here are born asleep
And I must leave them flowers of May
Before I wend my Christmas way

I give my harness bells three shakes
Then lift off through the drifting flakes
For I have many homes to seek
Where living children soundly sleep

And now the still born rest in peace
Beneath the Winter's downy fleece
I've all those promises to keep
For all the Saviour's dreaming sheep

The World is lovely - dark and deep
Above the lands where snow flakes sweep
But I have promises to keep
To all those angels sound asleep

And miles to go before I sleep
And myrrh to lay at Someone's feet.

Manatee

The manatee is the sailor's ugly mermaid
The seas fishy dough ball
The cow that swims on water-wings
Munching the salad dressing of the Everglades

The manatee is the seal's ugly sister
The blubbery girl that never gets to dance
With the double-breasted dolphins

Weeping under the water hyacinths
She is always looking for Cinderella's slipper
To fit her ugly flipper

She is always looking for her contact lenses
In the salty washing up.

Van Morrison's Astral Autumn Valentine

Amongst these Haunts of Ancient Peace
The seeker of the Veedon Fleece
Slips slowly down a Belfast street
Across the bridge where angels dwell
He lights upon a brown-eyed girl
Down Cypress Avenue she glides
A slim slow-sliding nubile type vibe
And he's onto her wavelength
He knows all the signs
Down the ancient old highway
Their life does unwind
Down by the pylons their love does unfurl
A Hyndford street man for his Tupelo girl
She gives him religion - she gives him the signs
And here in the garden the mystical wine
They dwell on the threshold - the stairway of time
Two souls in a mirror - two angels divine
The Queen of the Slipstream
She moves through the fair
And the sun it does shine
Through her corn-golden hair
On a gold Autumn day - through the bright Celtic ray
Through the Aryan mist - down the road there's a way
And they're into the mystic - the soul's caravan
No guru - no method they both understand
That the teacher of love is a beautiful man
And they're catching a fast train - the lion and the lamb
The Philosopher's Stone on Titania's hand.

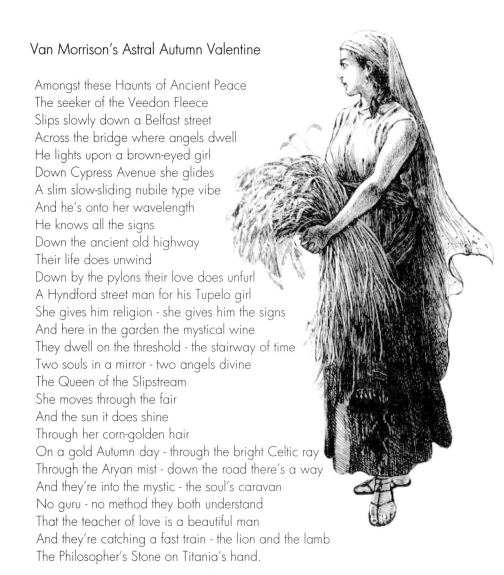

The Unicorn

The Unicorn is imagination's ivory lance
At night she wanders the Uffizi Gallery
And leaps into the Primavera
Always on the tip of your mind
She is the Poem you have been trying to find
Hidden only by a lack of vision
Visible only to children
Who fill the World with unfettered minds
And walk into wardrobes
To dance with lions.

Narwhals

Spiralling out of the Norse Eddas
Come the sea unicorns
Wave maned horses of the Northern ocean
Grail knights of the borealis
Blubbery Quixote's
Wielding their scrimshaw stalactites
Jousting on the margins of the Mappa Mundi.

First Fire

All of a sudden
The wood catches hold
And the first fire of encroaching Winter
Leaps the long length of chimney
To breathe smoke at stars
And warmth is borne like a wave
It flows into the bones as a vital wine
Then - for the first time since March
The sun is on the hearth
And the moon is at the window.

Georgian

The stream that wanders through our park
Is still a Greenwood stream at heart
Though tidied up for human tastes
And filled with thoughtless vandal's waste
It still seems an enchanted place
Where slowly now - at walking pace
I sometimes glimpse the Green Man's face
Suggestions of another sphere
Beyond the prams and cans of beer
A stream that swiftly tumbles through
This artificial country zoo
A stream that seems unsullied still
Despite the dam in mankind's will
Which gives to those who choose to look
A glimpse in Nature's secret book
A kingfisher that only flies
For those who have unblinkered eyes
Who know that "where there's muck there's brass"
A glimpse of our Edenic past
Before we put the railings round
And forced the Washbrook through the town.
It's still a place for inner calm
For soothing Nature's tranquil balm
But vandals cannot see the point
They'd rather sit and roll a joint
Or stick a needle in their arm
To feed on artificial charms
They only see an open sewer
That course past The Chef and Brewer
So miss the truly vital things
The brilliant flash of sapphire wings
That streaks on past their downcast hoods
Because they're lost in Dante's wood
The golden compass thrown away
That would have helped them on their way
And given them a fighting chance
To join the great anthemic dance.

The Gospel according to Stanley Spencer

In the beginning was the snowdrop
And the snowdrop was with God
And the snowdrop was God
Without the snowdrop was not anything made
That was made
In him was life
And the life was the light of men
And the snowdrop shineth in darkness
And the darkness comprehendeth it not

It was the end of the third day
So Stanley rested
Smiling at the Holy Flower

Then he planted his brushes in a rusty tin
Left them leaning by an oak tree's limb
And joined his disciples at the Cookham Inn.

Note on poem: The painter Stanley Spencer was noted for works which gave a sacramental flavour to his native village and many of his paintings picture scenes from the New Testament re-enacted on Cookham soil.

Hedgehog

Autumn's pin-cushion
The lovely moon pig
Is
Teasingly
Carelessly studded
With dead September leaves
As she shuffles down the catwalk
In an off the hedgerow number
Her body liberally sequinned
With hundreds of glittering fleas.

Mark Antony's Ode to Cleopatra's Bottom

Her buttocks swung from left to right
Two melons in a pair of tights

And as I watched the scrumptious maul
I knew that Rome would rise and fall

That Naples would be sacked by Gaul..

Those spheres I worshipped - day and night
Two beacons flaring - harbour lights

And when I think of them they sway
The one tolls night - the other day

And now I know - to my dismay
For Globes I gave the World away.

Stations of the Sun

January

In the middle of the New Year Field
Snowdrops lace
The scarecrow's boots.

February
Winter Celandines: Foxton Locks, Leicestershire

Fly wheels from Paley's golden watch
Carpet the rise
At Foxton Locks.

March
Battery farmed Daffodils: North Norfolk

Famous for fifteen flower vase minutes
Endless Xeroxed rows
Of Marilyn Monroes.

April
Memory Nearing Forty

In the blue jewellery box
My mother still keeps
My Spring teeth.

May
Beltane Kingfisher

A water sprite in dappled flight
A diamond cutter planing light
To clasp Titania's bluebell cloak
This lovely iridescent brooch.

June
Flanks of the White Horse, Uffington Val

Here...
Amongst his fetlocks
Iron age flowers still blooming.

July
Coniston Corrie

Clear as a bell
The slate rimmed lake
Tolls blue silence.

August

In the road
Late Summer leaves
Remind me of early deaths.

September

Between the branches of the sycamore
The wind is inking in
The Autumn stars.

October

Autumn comes
Even to the bonsai tree
Leaves fall gently on the fading geisha.

November
Child's Grave: Earlham Road Cemetery

Twenty years after that two day life
Someone is still laying flowers
Asking perfumed questions.

December
Aurora Borealis

Fingers of the Snow Queen
Plucking the harp
Of the stratosphere.

Praying Mantis

The Praying Mantis is part Heath Robinson
Part Edgar Allen Poe
It is all paper-clips and jaws
An origami dragon
Ralph Steadman's spider-graph of Satan
It is all green levers
And gossamer saws
It is all Vincent Price
And revolving doors
And Sweeny Todd is living in the apple of its eye
And Norman Bates is mother in its window on the sky
Where the Praying Mantis crunches on a struggling butterfly
And leafs through its chitinous bible
Of atrocious ways to die.

Lady of the Birches

For Maria Guerten, painter and tile maker
whose ashes were scattered at Dunwich
Suffolk amongst the birches she loved so much
by her partner Keith.

He cast her ashes hereabouts
Flung memories upon the wind
And now the pigment of her soul
Has mixed to make this picture whole
The potter has become the clay
The outer vessel falls away
And now she is inside the land
She painted with her living hand
She is the inscape of the earth
The rubric of this living church
Where sunlight slants through stunted birch
And picks its way amongst the dirt
To show the beauty of her works
Enfolded in enchanted earth.

The Irish Toucans: *For J. P. Donleavy*

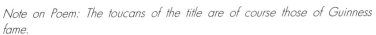

The toucans love the Irish brogue
And smoky pubs and panty hose
They really come here for the craic
These bright ceramic acrobats
They love to dodge the whirling flack
The hurling sound of ball on bat
For Dublin is their Summer home
They nest in haunts where writers roamed
The drayman finds them flying round
The turrets of the morning town
They break open his bottle tops
And guzzle Guinness on the rocks
The broody birds of Trinity
They cohabit in groups of three
They sing 'The Rose of Old Tralee'
Eat cockles - mussels by the sea
Then flock across a million garrets
As garrulous as Grimsby parrots
If Yeats had seen the toucans fly
Across a starry crowded sky
He would have dumped the swans at Coole
Have broken every bardic rule
And written of the toucan's flight
Round Maud Gonne's comely bedside light.

Note on Poem: The toucans of the title are of course those of Guinness fame.
J.P. Donleavy is one of my favourite un-pc novelists. Sadly many of his novels now appear to be out of print, although my love of literature was weaned on such alliterative titles as The Beastly Beatitudes of Balthazar B ...! Maud Gonne was the unrequited love of W.B. Yeat's life.

94

Life-Size Seated Angel: *Earlham Road Cemetery, Norwich*

An angel sits upon a grave
Her sculpted wings are slightly raised
And if you look into her eyes
The sorrow of the World's implied
She's waiting for our worlds to end
And every grave has such a friend
Wild leaves reach out around her head
Like something almost being said
They weave a wreath round every ledge
A halo for the dancing dead
If lips could speak - so carved in stone
She'd tell us we were not alone
We all have angels by our beds
They sit with us from birth to death
And if we ask they'll take our hands
And lead us to the promised land
And if we don't they'll still be there
To comfort us in our despair
I see this angel every week
But of my own I cannot speak
I only know that she is there
And runs her fingers through my hair
An angel sits upon a grave
Her sculpted wings are slightly raised
And as I gaze into her eyes
The wings of Isis open wide.

Mr Micawber's Kingfisher

Dressed in silks and fine brocade
Beau Brummell on the esplanade
His cut belies his true address
A bawdy house
A stinking crèche
A vomitorium
A mess
Flag iris round his doorbell hung
Cannot disguise the whiff of dung
Despite his Oscar Wilde attire
He does not live at dreaming spires
But just behind the toilet duck
Around the U-bend
In the muck
Where all the sticklebacks thrown up
All over Mrs Lady Luck
And all the little kingfish cheep
"We don't want stickleback this week!"
And all the bills lie in a heap
And no one gets a wink of sleep
Whilst on an angler's radio
They're playing Orinoco flow
As chamber pots all overflow
Into the river down below
"Next year my dear twill be the Ritz"
Says Mr Kingfisher in fits
"Next year my dear we'll cruise St Kitt's
Next year my dear we'll live like swifts…!"
"You're right" she says "We must persist
We must retrench - abstain - desist
We must pawn all our wedding gifts
And wait for all the clouds to lift
But until then there's you and I
The Kingfish and the open sky"
"You're right" she says - "my spirits lift"
And until then we have 'The Pitts'…!"

Jurassic Echinoid
Found Cromer Beach, June 2007

One hundred million years have passed
Since Echinodea breathed her last
And settled on the ocean floor
Beside the rotting ichthyosaur
But here - today - on Cromer beach
I found the Gorgon sculpted piece
A pin-cushion all turned to stone
A colander of pearly bone
A drifter on a tropic sea
In all her prickled finery
Now beached upon a colder strand
Amongst the North seas contraband
The Baltic amber - ice age tusks
The ambergris - all spermy musk
The rusted tins of lobster bisque
Requests for Desert Island Disks
The mermaid's purse - the belemnites
A lucky dip of earthly life
A geologic bouillabaisse
All served up by the springtime waves
And laid out by the tidal drag
Like fish upon a marble slab.

Late Spring Sanderlings
Overstrand Beach, North Norfolk, June 2007

They skitter-scatter on the sand
The sea chaff blown upon the strand
In imitation of the waves
They synchronize their swish displays
All plucked by some unseeing hand
And swept across the foam-flecked land
They echo one another's flight
God's small change
Spinning
In the light.

The Blue Tit's Nest: *For John Clare*

Her nest is made when moss abounds
All gathered from the splashy ground
And fashioned like a wattle ruff
All daubed with lovely bits of fluff
A wicker grail for brindled eggs
On which she broods inside our shed
Then feeds them when their beaks break through
Like crocuses amongst the dew
The parents flying back and forth
From East and South and West and North
With nuts and seeds and twitchy grubs
All garnered with instinctive love
Until the day the fledglings fly
And leave this woven lullaby
And when they'd flown I peeped inside
And found this dead chick on its side.

Larkinesque

When I see others - hand in hand
Entranced upon the Summer sands
I think of all the love I missed
Of all the girls I could have kissed
Now settled down in gilded hives
Corroded by their humdrum lives
The scent of grass and love is gone
As distant as a fairground song
Yet still I know that love was there
A promise in the English air
High Windows spilling hope and care
On Whitsun Weddings everywhere
But know that time has hurried on
That all that early hope has gone
And left me on this tidal flat
A loner in a battered hat
With nothing left to dull the pain
The anguish of this evening rain.

The Abyss: *For Alfred Lord Tennyson*

Beneath the place where sunlight's reach
Is staunched amongst the tropic deeps
Beneath the ocean's troposphere
We find gigantic chandeliers
Whose phosphorescent fungal cells
Illumine creatures drawn from hell
In sconces on great canyon walls
They light Poseidon's ghastly halls
Where creatures never dreamt by God
Extrude themselves from smoking pods
And drift and across the ocean floor
Great basilisks with blazing jaws
Who never see the haunts of men
Until their life releases them
To rise from their abysmal homes
And die upon the starlit foam.

Osprey

My castle is a mountain pine
My window on the West inclines

I am the Lord of river bends
The Fisher-King of mountain glens

I am the pendulum that swings
Across the loch with midnight wings

To pluck the salmon from his lie
Haul flapping silver through the sky

The last thing that the salmon sights
The priest who gives the final rights

I glory in my sweeping flights
I plunge across the Northern Lights.

The Sparkling Thrush: *For Thomas Traherne*
(With apologies to doubting Thomas Hardy)

I lent upon a coppice gate
When God was making hay
And Heaven's light made seraphs
Of the seagulls in the bay
The slender birch trees scored the sky
Like psalmist's silver lyres
And all mankind that vaulted night
Was rimmed by orbs of fire
The lands soft features seemed to me
The shape of God out leant
His throne the oak tree's canopy
The sky his sapphire tent
The ancient pulse of love and birth
Had blossomed in the sky
And every pilgrim on the earth
Seemed blessed as much as I
And then a voice arose among
The oak leaves overhead
In a full throated trumpet call
To resurrect the dead
A sparkling thrush - bright - plump and small
In pitch and perfect tune
Had chosen now to sing God's love
Beneath the harvest moon
Such joyful cause for outpourings
Of sweet angelic sound
Was written on the brightest wings
That glimmered all around
That I could see there shimmered through
His gorgeous - stained glass air
That blessed land through which he flew
And I was now aware.

Dormouse Triptych

The dormouse
Has made her winter billet
In the shape of the earth
Tucked her claws
Into the gloves of her ears
Turned her heart down
To a careless whisper
Outside the snow falls
In white epiphanies
And the cold sears all things
But the dormouse does not know
What Winter brings
A creature of three seasons
She blossoms with the flowers
Scurries through eternal Summer
Tip-toes into weeping Autumn
Climbs into the teapot of her harvest home
Dreams under the night light of the North Star.

Arse over Tit

Brazilians love their derrières
The English love their curves upstairs

I love the dark side of the moon
A peach that has a dusky bloom

I love the bottom - not the top
Perhaps I'm of Hispanic stock...?

I crave the far side in my mind
I keep abreast - I fall in line

But - underneath I pantomime
That loving bums is not a crime

A rearguard action when supine
Is heady as the finest wine

The frontal globes are pert - sublime
Pastiches of the ancient kind

The frontal globes are Guggenheims
But Heaven is a vast behind...!

Elephant

The great earth whale
With its curves of pearl
Is a swirl of grey
On the cusp of the morning
A brethren of blended shadow
A glorious mass of heaving Heaven
Lonely on the rim of the World
Calling to the planet
To save itself from idle treasures
The lathe tooled trinket
The hand carved toy
The smiling Buddha's carved jowls of joy
But soon the elephant itself
Sculpted from its own sacrifice
Hacked from its own bones
Will stride the mantelpieces
Of suburban homes
Forever mute to the ivory music
Of midnight guns
Quiet as the sun bleached skulls
That litter the mantelpiece of Africa.

Sloth

I like to hang for hours and hours
And contemplate the lovely flowers
The World's much better when its slow
And as the slowest I should know
There's too much rushing all around
There's too much volume
Too much sound
The jungle's filled with too much noise
There's hardly any equipoise
So - if you want a tip from me
Just join the sloth fraternity
Then hang around for hours and hours
And contemplate the lovely flowers...

Serket's Song

One of four tutelary deities whose outstretched wings
protect the canopic chest

I'm one of four who guard this shrine
I tend his heart as if it's mine

I'm tender in my carved embrace
My smile ensures sweet Amen's grace

I carry all his love and faith
Enshrined inside this wooden case

I am the watcher draped in gold
The keeper of this precious hold

Upon my head there rests a dove
The symbol of my timeless love

Three thousand years I've kept my watch
In sorrow for his grievous loss

In concert with my slender peers
We dance around the boy king's bier

We are the compass points of prayer
His soul in our eternal care

Within the circle of our wings
The Ka of Tutankhamen sings

Encircled by our timeless love
He smiles down from the stars above.

S.S.Guard; Auschwitz

"You go right and you go left
I have the power of life and death
I do not mind which way you go
For you to ask - for me to know
A Janus in my little cell
I am the Emperor of Hell
The bank clerk with a fountain pen
Filled with the blood of murdered men
Of women - children - rich and poor
I am the keeper of the door
Of homos - gypsies - mad and blind
I can be cruel - I can be kind
I started as a banker's clerk
Now murder is a work of art
You go right and you go left
And you to Mengele for tests
Your span is mine to re-assess
Your life is mine to dispossess
You are all numbers in my head
I add and then subtract the dead
I am the master you address
The scrivener of nothingness."

Snowdrops

There is a quiet strength about them
Gandhi kneeling in the road
Before the bulldozer of Imperialism
The man standing before the tank
In Tiananmen Square
American students filling rifles
With flowers
They are not angry with Winter
They just tell the truth
Wait - like a Burmese Boddhisvata
For the climate to change
They love what is right
The meltwater from the March hills
They prefer the method of the silent witness
White ink on a white page
Diamond sutras from the Blue Cliff Record
Bees of the invisible
Pollinating the earth with ineffable beauty
They are simply themselves
The frangible lights of this fractured world
Carillons pealing in teething woods
Baptists trailing the Lenten lillies
Prayer flags caught in the Green Man's beard.

Phone Head

I picked up the telephone
"No" - she said
"I'm not dead."
And all this time
I thought that I'd been writing letters
To a stone head
A basilisk of no emotions
Gazing out from hooded eyes
Across the shipwreck of our lives
"Let's meet" - she said
"I know a place of greater safety
It's a lovely island called friendship...!"
"Wonderful..." I replied
"I'll be right over...!"
I put down the telephone
Packed my griefs and my Ray-bans
Climbed aboard the Ra of the future
And sailed to Easter Island instead.

Juvenile Kingfisher - Late Summer

Bridge over stream, under Grand Union Canal aqueduct
Newton Harcourt, Leicestershire, 2007

Close up he's muted
His colours are sleeping
But then he takes flight
And a spectrum is beating
A Pharonic necklace with lazuli beading
A rose window lit by the sunset's last gleamings
And then he arcs down
And a rainbow is sweeping
To snatch up the silver
The swift stream is keeping
The lake lady's fingers extended in greeting
Excalibur's glint in the cool of the evening.

The Oldest Woman in France Remembers

"Merde...!
But he was rude
A ginger haired man
Reeking of absinthe...!

I sold him a tube of chromium yellow
Then he painted those sunflowers
...miserable fellow

And Toulouse - the crippled one...?
He was no better
He didn't want oils
Just a pack of French letters...!"

Khayyam's Cock - Up: *For Wendy Cope*

Awake...!
For someone in the bowl of night
Has had a slight disaster
With a mis-timed flight
And... oh the huntress
Like a beast has clasped
Her Sultan's rosy turret
In a fist of ice ...

Christmas Gift

What are the geese pulling
Through the frosted air...?
They are pulling the tides
And Autumn's hair
They are coaxing the moon
From its yawning lair
They are sweeping the snow
From the starlit stair
And escaping the jaws of the polar bear
What are the geese pulling
Through the frosted air...?
They are pulling Winter
On her painted sledge
They are leaving cobwebs
On a frosted hedge
They are sweeping Eastwards
Leaving springtime's pledge
And a glass of moonlight
On your window-ledge.

Yorkshire Tea - A Global Warming

Up on the fells
You often see
The Yorkshire fell maidens
Picking tea

It does seem strange
I must agree
To see these maidens
Picking tea
But Yorkshire is a hilly place
And tea does well on a mountain face

And Yorkshire wine is also nice
And olives here are half the price
As is Yorkshire basmati rice

I've heard that parkins going strong
Made by maidens in Ceylon
And hope that soon we'll see in cans
Esteemed black pudding from Rajasthan
Yorkshire pudding from Patagonia
And Wensleydale cheese from Outer Mongolia

The climate's changed up here you see
But Yorkshire folk miss tripe for tea

And though they like their Yorkshire tea
They'd prefer it from India

Naturally...!

114

Shamanic Dreams

It is as if a glacier has calved
And brought forth the living presence of the land
Or an Inuit child has made a snow bear
From the snow flakes of his thought
Which was absent in the morning
Leaving only tracks in the stillness

Yet somewhere his bear is moving
Loping under the borealis
A lonely thought in the greater loneliness
Somewhere his bear is waiting
Dreaming a white dream

Somewhere his bear is waiting
Dreaming the dreams of a bear
Dreaming the dreams of a child
Dreaming the dreams of them both

Quiet as a cat by a mouse hole
Dreaming a seal into existence.

Big Poem Hunter

The poet is trying to catch an animal
Silently he goes downwind
Armed only with a bag of metaphors
A roll of alliteration
Some flash bulbs of onomatopoeia

Now he loads the camera with unpredictable imagination
Takes aim
And fires a volley of sunlit words

Usually the animal gets away

But sometimes
Only sometimes
He processes the film
And finds the creature
Fixed in the developing tray
In beautiful - lyrical focus
Dressed in the poet's distinctive colours.

Pygmy Hippo: *Regency Park Zoo*

Small and black
Enchantingly fat

A bonsai hippo
Going slappity-slap

A pert but perfect submarine
A black-pudding floating
Through a Yorkshire man's dream

The charmingly wobbly
Cheeseburger fawn

A Nubian jelly
On a Regency lawn.

Hippo Haiku: *For Alison*

A sumo ballerina
Cavorting with her friends
Auditioning for Swan Lake in African D. M.'s.

Hippo of Troy: *For Les Dawson*

Because the hippo lost her brace
A grave-robbed smile
Adorns her face
She could have been a pageant queen
A cheer leader for football teams
Instead she drools from carmine lips
The face that sank a thousand ships.

Tutankhamen's Trumpet: *As heard on Radio 3 many years ago*

The breathing lips that pursed today
Blew all of cobwebbed time away
As music to a Pharaoh's ears
Came rolling down three thousand years
And crystal sets discerned the sound
That roused the Royal hunting hounds
And flushed the birds from swaying reeds
As plucked electrum fanned the breeze
A maiden bending on her knees
To kiss her archer and her liege.

Emporors

A flock of brooding styolites
Endure the great Antarctic night
For eighty days of absent light
They warm their eggs and give them life
What thoughts assail their penguin brains
Whilst huddled in the glacial rain
What gives them strength to carry on
With all their female penguins gone...?
They hum the incubation song
Spin Winter yarns to stoic throngs
Of leopard seals and killer whales
And ships entombed by Winter gales
Of starlight glistening through the hail
And mermaids sporting rhinestone tails
Of icebergs calving in the Spring
Whilst shuffling in their dismal ring
But when the final night is done
They hear the female's plangent song
Belisha beacons in full sail
They've waddled through the Winter gales
With nothing on their penguin minds
But thoughts of guardsmen left behind
And when they breast the final rise
The wind is full of penguin cries
As all across the frozen sea
There blooms a flightless symphony
The air redolent with the sound
Of penguins hatching all around.

Note on Poem: Styolites are named after Stilites a Christian hermit who began a craze for living an emaciated hermetic existence on top of long poles. People came to see him from miles around and he was one of the first Christian celebrities.!

A Mini Bestiary

A

Sea Anemone

I'm Cleopatra underwater
I'm Neptune's lissom
Rock pool daughter

I flower with each incoming tide
The faithful moon keeps me alive

Provides my breakfast - lunch and tea
Served by the hand maid of the sea.

B

Blackbird

The flautist with the golden beak
Who lulls you off to lovely sleep
Is singing in a nearby tree
And when you're tucked up – safe and sound
His melody drifts all around
A song that pours from Summer earth
Like pennies from a velvet purse
As - all around our sunset town
The blackbirds bring the curtain down .

C

Dream of the Cormorant Fisherman

In the night sky
My cormorant dives
Amongst shoals of stars.

D

Dormouse Dreaming

Curled up - like a pocket watch
The dormouse ticks
The dormouse tocks
Until its paws say five to Spring
For then the clock's alarm bell rings
And from a waistcoat's downy pocket
The March hare opens Winter's locket
To tell the dormouse that it's time
To wake up from this yawning rhyme.

E

Emperors

Glimpsed through Winter mists
A swathe of glass-blown orchids
A field of starlit chessmen
Glazed by the midnight sun.

F

Electric Cat Fish

A cat fish is useful for kick-starting cars
For shaving adaptors
And dim lights round bars
But – perhaps best of all is its use as a phone
With a fish in your ear you're never alone...!

G

Gecko

A delicate lizard
With sink plunging feet
The gecko can squirm over ceilings or seats
For the heavens are just as safe as a chair
When you're light as a feather
And velcroed ro air.

H

Sea Horse

*A pregnant pause
In a sea of troubles*

*A glass-blown fern
In a stream of bubbles*

*A chess board knight
On a looking glass lawn*

*A mandolin prancing
To Neptune's horn.*

I

Impala

*Bouncing on African springs
The impala is impelled
By the golden scent of death
To float away from slouching danger
In blazing fawn parabolas.*

J

Jellyfish

*A pulsar
Winking in the night
A distant fairground's fairy lights
The blooms of Neptune floating free
The hanging gardens of the sea.*

K

September Kingfisher

Trafficlightsblurringinautumnrain.

L

Lampreys

*Freshwater 'slugs'
With watch parts for teeth
Lampreys were served
At large monarchs' feasts
But - ever since then
Their charm has declined
And no one dines out
With lampreys in mind.*

M

Mammoth

*A fork lift truck
In an Afghan coat
Orson Wells in an ice cream float
The deepest Winter you could dream
The snow plough of the Pleistocene.*

N

Narwhal

*The narwhal is an ivory corkscrew
Opening millions of gallons
Of Arctic Beaujolais.*

O

Oyster

The oyster is an unwilling jeweller
Who uses an alchemist's gland
To spin soothing Fabergé worlds
Round aching grains of sand.

P

Pelican

If a Pelican
Why can't a Parma ham
Or an Elvis fan
Or Desperate Dan...?

Q

Resplendent Quetzal

Atahuelpha's Inca crown
The Aztec priesthoods dressing gown
The sadness of a thing of love
All stolen in the name of blood.

R

Stamp of Christ

The robin is Nature's symbolic flame
Impervious to wind and rain
Transcendent on a frozen pail
The stamp of Christ on Advent mail.

S

Scorpion

A question mark above the sand
A shepherd's crook
A poison gland
The sleek hull of a barbed Trireme
A Grecian floating war machine
And at the front a pair of claws
To feed the beasts revolving jaws.

T

The Darkling Thrush
For Jesus, aged 4, Nazareth Elementary

This is the bird that Jesus made
Whilst playing in the second grade
From claggy earth - the darkling sky
A snatch of Mary's lullaby.
The glad thing was he made him wing
Across to Dorset carolling
The sad thing was he made him sing
About the gladness God would bring
But left him by the coppice gate
Where Doubting Thomas lost his faith.

U

Unicorns

A silver stallion's lance of light
Is flashing in the Arden night
And angels from the seven realms
Are greaved and metalled
Armed and helmed
They come with love light in their eyes
And on their unicorns they ride
A cavalcade of Kings and Queens
Across the fields of children's dreams.

V

Velociraptor

I am the streetwise dinosaur
With gold - capped teeth in either jaw
And on the urban jungle's floor
My word is might my word is law
I am the streetwise dinosaur
I sushi words uncooked and raw
And on the urban jungle's floor
These words become an extra claw
And on the urban jungle's floor
I use these words to go to war.

W

Wren for all Seasons

A thimble
Borne on Autumn leaves
A snuffbox
Filled with Summer seeds
Tom Thumb
Perched on Springtime's palm
A haiku
For a Winter psalm.

X

Xiphias Gladius: *Swordfish*

Errol Flynn with added fins
Pinocchio with water wings
A jousting knight beneath the foam
Neptune's barber when in Rome.

Y

Yak

Rancid butter floating
In well stewed tea
Is no great aid
To he image of the yak
Who would I'm sure prefer
To have chocolate made
From her butter fat...!

Z

Zebu

A Brahmin bull
The Zebus is also untouchable
It is India's king of sacred beauty
Very heavy - if slightly effete
It is the dewlapped Shiva that wanders the streets
Rising above the common herd
It is the alabaster herbivore
Dispenser of Wyrd
And birds take rides on its marble back
Whilst beggars in tattered hessian sacks
Make way for these Gods who lumber past
(Whilst McDonald's executives look on aghast)
To drink from the sacred Bramaputra
And dream under Siddhartha's crumbling stupa.

Swift

No undercarriage to speak of
Just the tenterhooks
The vestiges of grasping
As we in the womb have momentary gills
To remind us of its earthbound beginnings
Its old material clingings
Before it became a trainee angel
Barnstorming the ionosphere.

Ozymandias 11

I felt you were my other half
The shadow on a Summer lawn
Which - when I looked up
Showed me why
My present half was really born

I felt that we were of a piece
A sculpture joined by common clay
That - though it passed through many forms
Had ruled a kingdom in its day

I felt that time would find us out
Re-site us on a brilliant hill
But though the forger plied his art
He did not have sufficient skill

So now we lie in distant lands
Our pieces claimed by different hands
And - by the plinth where we once stood
The shards of love stretch far away.

The Watchful Sandman

Love fades
Like forgotten telephone numbers
The digits - once so meaningful
Are blurred within a week

I put your photograph in the bin
Sifted my soul from yours
Took what could be recycled
To the memory bank up the hill

But even the cheerful dustman
Can't remove a dune of grief

So I planted it with the marram grass
Of fortitude
Erected the groynes of adversity

Then I left it with the watchful sandman
By the ribs of a Summer creek.

Owl

Two great plates of light
An undercarriage of intricate butchery
And a beak for tearing the hearts from hares
The owl is prowling across its demesne

Dreaming from the barn
It is gliding to harvest its tithe of velvet

Later
Far down
Far down below
Like a moth drawn irrevocably
To the light of life
A leveret is smelt in the infrared
Warm blooded in the hooting night-finder
Then the pendulum descends
In swathes of silence

Two great plates of night
An undercarriage of intricate butchery

Then the harpy's gleaning
And the tithe is screaming.

Blackbird Jam in January
Walking the dog at midnight

Despite the cold
The inclement weather
The blackbirds under the wind-picked moon
Sing their midnight madrigals
All birds of a frozen feather
In the bare ruined choirs
Of the roofless Winter shires
They congregate together.
Vivaldi's plainsong Winter page
Is lit with crotchets on a stave
A magic box of Mozart flutes
To thaw the snowdrops at the root
To usher in the budding shoots
And all the sleeping springtime fruits
And so - above the frosty thistles
Above the warblers and the missels
Above the nightingale's epistles
I love God's cheerful penny whistles.

Incident at the Tomb of Arimathea

"Are you the keeper of this place?"
Said Mary to the shrouded face

"I am the gardener"
Said the man
"The one who tills the promised land
I am the steward of the earth
The keeper of this hallowed turf
I am the one who tends the vines
Who turns the water
Into wine
I am the tiny mustard seed
That flowers into mystic trees
I am the shepherd of the earth
The wet nurse at each lambs new birth
I am the one who catches men
Who hooks
Then throws them back again
I am the shepherd of the stars
Of all the souls both near and far
I am the bard who writes the plays
In which you pass your doubting days
I am the one who wrote the script
Produced - directed
Starred in it
I fashioned you from earthly clay
To be with me upon this day
And who do you say that I am...?"

"I know" she said

"The Son of Man."

Made of Stars: *For Richard Jefferies*

The gospels made at Lindisfarne
Are rich essays on Nature's charms
But painted gospels of the Word
Have nothing on a singing bird
Who fills the wood with fluted psalms
And leaves all human notes becalmed
Our artifice delights our eye
But cannot paint a Summer sky
The lark ascending with the dawn
Above the flaxen fields of corn
Our human art is but pretence
A pantomime of real events
The poem on this printed page
Is like a bird inside a cage
Which sings - but like a clockwork toy
That's wound up for our selfish joy
Open the doors - let life escape
The riches of our Globe's estate
Are there for all to be enjoyed
Our human arts are only boys
And when we grow up wisdom brings
The wish to cast off childish things
And enjoy things for what they are
A Celtic gospel made of stars.

Man Eater: *For Rudyard Kipling*

He came - like Grendel in the night
A phantom on the edge of sight
He ghosted from the misty ghats
Through temples where Lord Krishna sat
And took the people one by one
Because he was an outcast son
And found such humans easy meat
Beneath the great Lord Krishna's feet
The jungle drums could not defy
A leopard with such midnight eyes
Who could so clearly see his prey
Though darkness covered Mandelay
And doors were shuttered - blinds were drawn
Against another blood-soaked dawn
Where wailing from the rose red shrines
Said death had spoken one more time
And left a piece of butchered meat
Beneath Lord Krishna's time worn feet
For eight long years the creature roamed
Made Kashmir's skirts his killing zone
He drifted in and out of myth
Left paw prints in the mountain mist
Until the hunter tracked him down
And blasted him on Kashmir's crown...
Despite a tale so plain and stark
The burning pyre of human hearts
The man eater has left his mark
His killing fields a National Park
Established by the very man
Who later learned to stay his hand
And let the wild things wander free
Beneath the Bodhi Gaya Tree.

Magi

Great shadows on a lapis sky
The potentates glide softly by
Encrusted with the emerald earth
They voyage to glimpse a Virgin birth

Across the deserts flood of hours
They ply their ships past rose red towers
On palanquins of sumptuous hide
A pearl above their lustrous guide

And every Christmas time they come
With blazing gifts for Mary's son

Three gilded kings from lands afar
To crown the shepherd of the stars.

A Panda gives The Reith Lectures

The panda has taken off his spectacles
He is rather hot and flustered
He is giving the Reith Lectures on endangered species
He drinks a glass of bamboo juice
Shuffles his papers
"Gosh - isn't he cute !" says a pubescent white rhino
In an ill fitting - double-breasted
Mike Tyson sort of suit
"I wish he'd been around when I was here."
Says a ghostly Quagga
"I hope he'll put in a hoof note for me."
"I'm sure he will dear..." says a kindly giraffe
Who has temporarily entangled her earrings in the lighting rig
Meanwhile lion bars rustle - warthog sneeze
Wildebeest bellow
An owl begins to hoot...
"Ahem." says the panda
Glowering benignly
"I would like to begin..." says the panda
Replacing his spectacles
"By reading a paper on our most endangered species"
Well the necks all turn
Searching for this marvellous - cuddly creation
This wonder of the World
This great - endearing brute
But - to the consternation of the panda
The human has already left
With the animals in pursuit.

Summerlands: *In memory of David Sainsbury and for his wife Ursula Sainsbury and family*

The pier stalks out on cast iron legs
The seagulls cartwheel overhead
The old boats painted blue and red
Trawl sweet crabs for the boiling shed
The gorse upon the cliffs in bloom
The foxgloves through the woods are strewn
And on the freshly minted sand
Old lovers stroll past - hand in hand
Retirement beckoned long ago
When land-locked woods were full of snow
When love was young and children came
To walk the flint walled Norfolk lanes
And take the path along the dyke
In Norfolk's misty morning light
To fish for crabs in charming Wells
And walk the beach in search of shells
To fill delighted childhood eyes
With endless watercolour skies
To watch the seals off Blakeney's coast
From lovely - clinkered fishing boats
And hear the bittern's booming cry
Amongst the reeds where Titchwell lies
To take the train from Sheringham
Across the fields of Poppyland
Eat sandwiches where mines once lay
To keep the German hordes at bay
Drink pop where Nelson had his grog
And raise a glass for Ransome's mob
Who - wrapped up in their Norfolk bunks
Keep quiet about the captain's trunk
To breakfast here at Overstrand
And watch the tractors on the sands
Pull out the graceful crabbing boats
And dunk them all in Shakespeare's moat
And now their children's children come
Enraptured by the Norfolk sun

To walk the same old paths and lanes
And hear the greylag's wild refrain
To comb the endless miles of shore
Beside the ocean's muted roar
It is a landscape handed on
To generations yet to come
Bequeathed to those who've yet to find
The treasures in a childhood mind
The natural things that reconnect
Our island nation's warp and weft
It is a seascape in the head

The land-locked sailor's daily bread
A picture postcard in the mind
To take out in the wintertime
A set of magic lantern slides
That bring to us on memories tides
The flotsam of the seaside fair
The jetsam of that love affair
Played back in peaceful reverie
Against the backdrop of the sea
A place to beachcomb far inland
Turn memories with time worn hands
And place them on the mantelshelf
Bright seashells beached amongst the Delft
But now the lovers second home
Is reclaimed as their very own
They live beside the booming sea
Their backcloth brushed by memories
As - underneath the Norfolk skies
They play out their remaining lives
And welcome children they once named
And grandchildren with current flames
To walk these old familiar lanes
To play the old familiar games
And watch the geese fly though the air
To Summerlands they all can share.

Pike Quartet

1

Under the arch of brick and stone
Hannibal Lecter waits to phone
The shivering stickleback
Home alone...

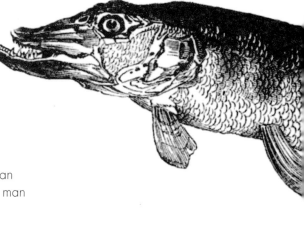

2

Glinting in the lake
A votive offering
A mere monster
Grendel's ghastly outrider
A lone marauder from a rabid clan
The stickleback children's bogey man
Jack the Ripper's gas lit breath
A stalker in the watercress.

3

Sculling under the sun dappled bracken
The Texas Chainsaw Massacre
Waiting to happen...

4

Winter's megalithic icicle
Dark star at the heart of the solstice lake
King of ghostly swords
Heron eyed cutlass
Stickleback widower
Long ship of shield walled malice
Nemesis of dace
Macbeth's dripping dagger
Floating in Celtic space.

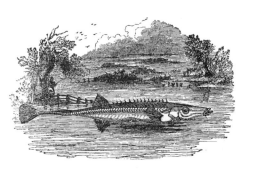

The Museum of Love

In the Museum of Love
There are many curiosities
Terrible mistakes line the shelves
In their cloudy jars
They are all labelled
All accounted for
And - in the Egyptian Room lie the relationships
He tried to save
To ardently embalm beyond their rightful graves
None of course are living in this catacomb of roses
Nobody ever comes…
Nobody ever visits…
The doors are sealed with lips of wax
Once cannot gain an audience by letter - phone or fax
For the Museum of Love is not open to the public

Every so often a poem shines a torch
The curator makes his rounds
But the lips of wax are sealed
Osiris has not risen
And the Museum of Love is silent
There is nothing to report.

Yorkshire Farmhouse Window: *For James Herriot*

The only painting on the wall
Is a work by God entitled 'Spring'
Who also has three others
Under dust sheets in the wings
They come out every year
And are hung successively
But each year they are different
Though they frame the selfsame tree
And each time the light changes
It's God's Yorkshire that we see.

Giraffe: *For Roy Campbell*

Warily he drinks
In camouflaged communion
Arching the neck with its seven bones
He prays to the gunpowder river
Curtseying his quilted hide
Defenceless in his clumsy elegance
Like a Samurai without his sword
He swings
Beautifully low
To sip Kilimanjaro's melted snows
Lamarck's living ladder
He browses in the higher reaches
A question mark on the rolling plains
He glooms - like a gentle watchtower
Engulfed in thundering wildebeest flames
A sentry of the Serengeti
He watches over Africa's darkening ocean
Like a magic carpet
To the sunrise hours
Like a living - breathing
Periscope of flowers.

Snow Leopard: *For Peter Matthiessen*

Snow shoe soft the leopard goes
Across the passes prana flows
The Buddhist searches for a koan
And finds the leopard all alone
A diamond sutra in the night
Nirvana glimpsed by candlelight
The prayer flags flutter in the wind
The prayer wheels turn - the chant begins
Whilst - high above the leopard's eyes
Are filled with Himalayan skies
And far below the yak trail winds
Across the foothills of the mind
As one hand claps the mystery sound
Of leopard laughter swirls around
A creature who cannot be caught
By any rational train of thought
But slips beyond the bounds of time
Escapes the couplets of this rhyme
Eloping from the ties that bind
Into the mountains of the mind.

The Tortworth Chestnut

I am the oldest tree I know
My forbears died out long ago
And now I gaze out from the fronds
Methuselah from Angkor Thorn
A face that's seen a thousand springs
Bring vernal life to ancient limbs
And crown me with a thousand crowns
That every Autumn tumbled down
I've watched the children gather round
The pig nuts rattle to the ground
I've watched the moots of Saxon kings
Betrothals made with golden rings
Withstood the great Armada storm
That followed bowls upon the lawn
I've seen the Pilgrim Fathers go
Have watched the Round Heads pass below
Have seen the troops that Churchill sent
Cross Salisbury Plain with fixed intent
I've stood here - swaying since my birth
A Gog Magog of massive girth
A grizzled knight of Greenwood mirth
A Falstaff rooted in the earth....
I knew a birch queen long ago
Who danced with me amidst the snow
But she has gone - like all my friends
To feed the hearths of long dead men
Who've taken all my woods away
For ships and God and new mown hay
For mills and steam and motorways
To leave me seated on my throne
A king without his stately home
Abandoned here - a standing stone
To hold the stars up on my own.

Note on poem: The Tortworth chestnut, reputedly well over 1000 years old stands in a small sacred grove, just 5 minutes walk from the busy M5 as it wends its way to Bristol. Referred to throughout its later history as "that grand old chestnut" there is no doubt that it is one of the oldest and most venerable trees in the whole of the British Isles.

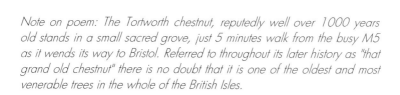

Migrating Swallows

Sycamore seeds dipped in lapis lazuli
Mackerel who've gained their wings
Errant notes from a Summer chorus line
Coat-hangers for the Autumn wind.

Autumn into Winter

It's now that Autumn edges in
The halberd of a Greenland king
A Viking ship of tumbled storms
Of Danegeld flung on frosted lawns
The sadness of a curlews cry
A throng of swallows spilling by
The golden torc of harvest moons
Of suppers spread in fire lit rooms
The silence of the standing stones
Whilst all around the North Wind moans
A glass of Summer by my bed
The wild geese creaking overhead.

13 ways of looking at a Kingfisher: *For Wallace Stevens*

Blue water flame
Test pilot of the Test
Shimmering spirit level of the glimmering Greenwood
Fan of Newtonian feathers
Hopkin's Seraphim
Flickering compass needle of our padlocked Eden
Druid's rush light
Litmus of evening loveliness
Little match girl's lodestar
Beau Brummell's river gambler
Isaak Walton's artful dodger
Tutankhamen's funeral necklace
Barnes Wallace skimming stones
On the Ocean of Tranquility.

Fiddler Crab: *For Nigel Kennedy*

The fiddler crab has eyes on stalks
And a claw so large it can hardly walk
It lives amongst the mangrove swamps
Where the David Attenborough yomps
And can often be seen at evening's end
Serenading its mud skipping friends
With a Cajun Stradivarius.

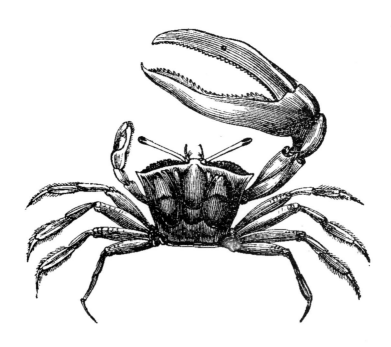

Beachcombers

Walking in each other's minds
Along the beach
We hope to find
Something that will tell us why
Love drifted off
And left us blind

Walking in each other's minds
Across our lives
We hope to find
A bottle with an ancient rhyme
That tells us why
We were unkind

And walk along this shell lined shore
In search of pearls we had before

The tide drifts out
And leaves us dry
We dream beneath a capsized sky

And walk inside each other's minds
Wishing we had been more kind.

Measuring the Moon: *For Brian Patten*

I gave you a haiku
You said it was beautiful
But you also said it wasn't long enough

So I gave you this ball of string
And asked you to measure the length of its beauty

Then I begged you to sit in an Autumn room
And measure the beauty of the harvest moon

(It was then that you gave me those seventeen kisses
A haiku you dreamt up whilst drying the dishes.)

Harvest Mouse in the Moon

Inside a crow's nest made of grass
He sways upon a barley mast
A puffball on an Autumn sea
The moon caught in the wicker trees.

Koala Calypso - or "What's de rush.,?!"

For Nick Park; to be read aloud, Caribbean style

Koala he move very slow
He never have too far to go
He like to sleep much of de time
Siesta help him to unwind
He chew de mighty menthol weed
De Eucalyptus help him breathe
De ganja of deze southern climes
It help him chill out all de time
He look up wiv his moon wide eyes
Wiv pudgy nose inspect de skies
He sleep above de guzzlin cars
His hammock slung beneath de stars
He don't go no place in a rush
He love his life - he want no fuss
He never get all down and blue
Just sip a glass of Malibu
And watch de Sheila's surfin through
Whilst blokes sweat on de barbeque
An easy life is all he ask
A stroll in Melbourne's gentle parks
But Mr K a sleepy head
So... mostly he just stay in bed...!

Me and Joni Mitchell

Blue...
I remember Blue
And only Joni Mitchell knew
She was the one who helped me see
She also had the blues like me
It was a secret that we shared
Along with kaftans - spliffs and flares
I listened and I knew she cared
That broken hearts could be repaired
That parking lots could be displaced
That trees could save the human race
We'd put away our café pain
And drive to Paris in the rain
Amelia would fly again
Up to the clouds Aegean blue
Along with pretty Peggy Sue
We'd help to make the World anew
I listened and believed it true
That love would find the chosen few
Along with every student who
Played Joni Mitchell...
Feeling Blue.

Waiting to Scramble
Garden Nest box, Poppy Close, June 2006

Great tits nesting here
In the spice-box of earth
A clamour of little anvils
A broth of beseeching beaks
A pubescent crèche of cacophonous cheeps
The parents flying in and out
Of the circle of light
Endlessly returning to the raucous commotion
The bird-brained boot-camp
Of a brood in motion
Endlessly returning
To the fire-box of nature
The sleep-over to end all sleep-overs
Until the day the school bell rings
The Coot Club signals
Here comes Summer…!
And greenhorn spitfires earn their wings.

Cuckoo Chick

He is the feathered Trojan horse
The gate crasher with no remorse
An orotund - unscripted guest
Who brings *fowl* murder to the nest
A doppelganger in the crèche
A foundling who is truly blessed
Then snatches all the silver spoons
From all his siblings - making room
For England's African imposter
This Jabberwock sweet warblers foster.

Maps and Dreams:
For Hugh Brody

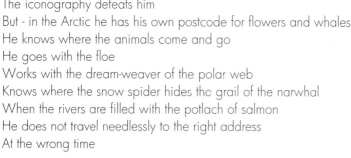

An Inuit is quickly lost
Amongst the cliffs of London
The iconography defeats him
But - in the Arctic he has his own postcode for flowers and whales
He knows where the animals come and go
He goes with the floe
Works with the dream-weaver of the polar web
Knows where the snow spider hides the grail of the narwhal
When the rivers are filled with the potlach of salmon
He does not travel needlessly to the right address
At the wrong time

The streets of ice are always changing
The whale road of Summer is closed in Winter

There is a time and a place for every purpose under Heaven
A time to sew - a time to reap
A time for giving - and a time to keep

The map of the Inuit cannot be folded in a pocket
Or kept like a charm in a silver locket
The dreams of the landscape cannot be bought
They are a tapestry of changing lights
A Bestiary of the polar mind
Illuminated by different animals
At different times

The land is bountiful in due season
And everything appears for a different reason

(In the palantir of the shaman
The caribou can now be seen on the distant shores of thought
Walking the whale road in their thousands).

151

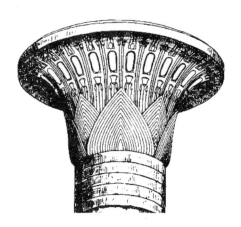

Aten...?

A child
Caught between the clashing rocks of ideologies
A sheep returning to the fold of Karnak
Under cover of religious darkness
The sun rolled up with the bed linen
One true God - hidden amongst many
Hands of light on his childhood throne.

Galapagos Tortoises

The giant tortoises are making love
Like slowly excited buildings

They have been sending each other flowers
For over forty years
But - only in the last forty months
Have they started gigantically courting
And shedding Churchillian tears

"I like the look of her...!"
Said one tortoise in eighteen ninety seven
But he didn't get round to asking her out
Till nineteen hundred and eleven
By which time she'd found someone else
A brash - Edwardian fast mover

It took him thirty years
To woo her slowly back

And only now have they finally closed
The forty year - five yard gap.

I am a Camera: *For Patrick Lichfield*

He was a man of light and shade
The lens through which the Sixties played
He was a master of his craft
Daguerreotype now seen as art
Although he was of Royal stock
He mucked in with the common lot
He partied with the common herd
A peacock amongst cockney birds
The focus of his life was framed
By apertures of cars and planes
But light was where this Magus played
He captured it on different days
In all its bright and brilliant ways
The photons from our distant sun
Were caught on time's revolving drum
Then wound back from his magic spool
As Madeleine's of karmic jewels
The light that flooded through his glass
Gave back to us our fleeting past
Pirelli girls and Royal scenes
A crocus from a Snowdon dream
Beatle's fans and Georgie Best
Sassoon - a cut above the rest
Ascot - Aintree - Derby day
The Jet Set snapped on holiday
Twiggy and the Rolling Stones
The age before the mobile phone
The light that plays across this land
Was captured by his dancing hands
But now the shutter of his mind
Has fallen for the final time
He finds he's dancing in the light
Photographer of Paradise.

Grumpy old Coelacanth: *For me...!*

Well adapted - perfect fit
The fish who hasn't changed a bit
An ancient rocker bucks the trend
The Status Quo just never ends
The five bar blues - the three chord riff
He really is a queer old fish
When asked out by an ancient flame
He said "The Song remains the Same..."
He does not have a face book site
His blog is set in lino type
He does not text - prefers to write
(His friends are mostly Trilobites)
The modern world is over hyped
His sympathies are quite Luddite
He still prefers the printed word
Etheric text is just absurd
He still loves Genesis and Floyd
All modern music's just a noise
And as for Darwin's evolution
For him the theories no solution..!
He cannot change habitual ways
When every eras Groundhog day
Immutable he seems to be
A species stuck at half past three
A creature old as all the stones
That calcified his parent's bones
A fogy old as Father Time
He still prefers the malmsey wines
He pedals round the ancient clock
A living fossil on the block
He does not care for modern trends
Edwardian he scarcely blends
Still cycling on his penny farthing
Amongst the mackerel and the marlin.

Note on Poem: The discovery of the Coelacanth, dragged up in a trawler's nets off the coast of South Africa in the late 1930's was one of the most amazing zoological stories of the 20th, or indeed any other century.

After much publicity another specimen was finally hooked off the Comores islands and the Coelacanth, which was considered to have died out millions of years ago was once again revealed to an astonished populace across the world as one of only a few creatures to merit the term 'Living Fossil' The tale is recounted in J.L.B. Smith's (the world famous ichthyologists) marvellous book - 'Old Fourlegs'.

Scarecrow

The scarecrow
Swings
In the rain drenched field
A creature made of roots and wheels
Who cannot think or hear or feel
And yet there's something in his stare
That makes me think there's someone there
A sentinel as pilgrims wend
A Janus as four seasons blend.

Bust of Nefertiti: *For H. Rider Haggard*

Your eyes of Kohl
Your feline gaze
The hands of light
The Aten praised
The great eternal catwalk queen
Iconic Sphinx for magazines
You gaze out from Armana's frame
Ayesha licked by tongues of flame
As subtle as a faint perfume
That drifts across the ancient dunes
You dream amongst the Winter mists
Of Akhenaten's springtime kiss
Though all the robes of time are frayed
Your cartouches defaced - erased
You live inside this statue still
The Ka of Bast's immortal will
The smile that lights up every age
And makes all men your willing slaves.

Note on poem: The bust of Nefertiti, surely one of the most beautiful women who ever lived was discovered in Tuthmoses, the sculptors's workshop in the ruins of Armana the heretical city of the sun founded by Nefertiti's husband the renegade Pharaoh Akhenaten who established the world's first monotheistic religion, the worship of the sun disc. Nefertiti's bust now resides in The Egyptian Museum in Berlin. H. Rider Haggard the Norfolk squire who wrote the celebrated adventure novels, King Solomon's Mines She and Ayesha surely had a figure such as Nefertiti in mind when he penned his romantic adventures.

Sea Henge

Seaweed cloaked the emerald man
The underwater pipes of Pan
This Yggdrasil off Norfolk's coast
Defended by its emerald moat
But - once it stood astride a ley
Before the moon queen had her way
And drowned this palisade of winds
Entombed this wooden henge of kings
Which drank the light of solstice day
Before the moon swept kings away.

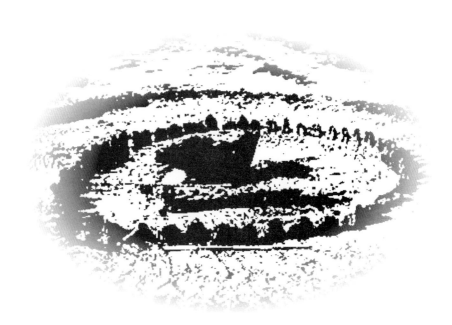

X

From an idea by Bilbo Dunion

Note on poem: Anyone feeling sad at the loss of the X's will be heartened by one of the roof bosses in Norwich Cathedral. The bosses are unique to Norwich and depict the whole Bible story in beautiful mediaeval vignettes and if you were to look up directly above the main altar you will see Noah's ark, Mr and Mrs Noah + assorted animals but, more to the point, jutting out of the aft of the vessel you will be delighted to see a Xunicorn…!

Before the flood there were many X's of both sexes
Xephons and Xaviers
Xengongs and Xuts
Xephers and Xengers
Xerods and …
Well the list went on… as they do
But someone at the ark made a Kakfkaesque error
And the X's were left to the rage of the weather
And Noah looked out from the poop of the ark
To the part of the alphabet lost in the dark
"Damn" said Noah
"I've got A's and B's, U's and V's
I've got them all doubled to the nineteenth degree
But the X's are lost to the Gilgamesh foam
And the alphabet's short of the X's we've known
The Xephods and Xaegars
Xagrabs and Xits
The Xentaurs and Xunicorns with the ivory bits"
And Noah cursed on - as he did but to no avail
As the ark was tossed in the forty day gale
Until - on the fortieth day the birds returned
The waters subsided
And the earth from the sea was once more divided
Then a rainbow blazed over Mount Ararat
And a Bestiary poured from the ark's wooden flaps
The J's and the P's
The Y's and the T's
The marvellous M's and ethereal G's
But - of the X's
Only silence
And pages torn from the bestial ledger
"No more" said a somewhat shame-faced Noah
"Will the X's give us such unbridled pleasure
I've just gone and ditched a planetary treasure
Shucks…!"
Then he went off with Ham to get heartily pissed
And the X's sank into colourful myth
A letter dropped from the bestial tree
Such Xotic creatures
Lost in the sea.

Bats

Match box night monsters
Bats shave past you
Antennae bristling
Painting the swerving landscape
With brushes of shadowy noise
For - inside their valve crammed heads
Night is lit by ultrasound
As they tune into the evening
To feed on radio dragonflies
That flicker across their wavebands
Like angels dressed in echoes.

Shape-shifter

A dream of Avebury, after viewing a painting
at the Sainsbury Centre, Norwich

I walked beyond the painting's frame
To stand amongst the ancient stones
And felt the iron age stain my veins
Beside a tumulus of bones

The painted wind beat on my head
The air was filled with primal power
And as the sun sank in the West
A figure climbed a painted tower

He turned towards the setting sun
And then he raised a hawthorn wand
And as I watched he changed his song

The Druid blurred... became a swan.

hUnny I Luv U

The eskimos hav 18 difrent names for snow
And todays snow wazn't like any snow I now
But – in the absense of an eskimo
Piglet and I hav decided to call it

Snow…!

The missticks hav 18 difrent names for luv
And todays luv waznt like any luv I new
But … in the absence of a wizer pooh
Piglet and I hav decided to call it
hUnny with a Kapital U…!

The Marriage of the Sun and Moon

For Douglas and Emily's union in the Jubilee Scout Field,
Norwich, a Fine City
7th August 2004

The energies of Yin and Yang
Are flowing from your entwined hands
The palette of your separate souls
Has mixed to make this picture whole
You once were joined at nature's source
Then - sundered through the eons coursed
The template of your separate lives
Was drawn beneath the starlit skies
And as you ploughed your separate arcs
The stories of your lives were marked
By passages through foreign lands
And journeys clasping other hands
The lessons of your love were forged
By wounds sustained in other wars
But - through it all your separate streams
Held memories of a common dream
The memory of a perfect love
Was mirrored in the stars above
And now the confluence has come
The marriage of the moon and sun
You each have found the other's hearth
And flames rekindled from the spark
Have joined the Niles both blue and white
In cataracts of sweet delight
You each now have each others rings
As memories of your common spring
You recognize your common cause
The ancient link has been re-forged
The heads and tails of love now meet
The circle here is now complete.

Note on Poem: It was Plato who first suggested the idea of perfect hermaphrodite forms, sundered at time's beginning who then spent the rest of eternity traversing the universe's long and winding Karmic road in search of their respective soul mates. The Chinese circular symbol of Ying and Yang suggests the perfect form produced by this symmetrical blending of male and female energies.

163

Badger: *For Pollyanna Pickering and Anna - Louise*

Painted with strokes of moonlight
The badger shuffles from the dark
Like a part of the dark advancing
The night sky caught in ambling time-lapse.
Stars spark from his town lit eyes
As this confederate of the constellations
This charcoal woodsman
Snuffles down the path between dusk and dawn
Melting with the morning
Like night fog
Lifting.

57 Ways of looking at Ted Hughes

You cannot bottle old Ted Hughes
As Pagan man or Morning Dew
As chutney or as Boots Home Brew
For he was morning - noon and night
A roe deer on a motorbike
And all of England's Season Songs
Were written with his magic wand
He's like the weather - always new
The rain - the wind - the lovely view
And all our green and troubled land
Is found in poems Hughes has canned.

Avocets

A wheeling flock of black and white
They flicker in the Minsmere light
Sweet birds in little cocktail numbers
Such emblematic Suffolk tumblers
They sweep across the harbour buoys
Like Aubrey Beardsley's clockwork toys
Alighting with their upswept beaks
To dibble in the silver creeks
Then perch upon their sapphire stilts
Like anchorites above the silt.

A Land Rover's Valentine:
Discovered in the wanted columns of Auto Trader

Right…
I'm a
Sixteen valve
Four wheel drive
Souped up
Diesel-powered
Trans-global
Off - road
Metal mercenary

HARD AS NAILS

Angry

(lonely)

Battered

(sad)

Looking for a small mini

…to love.

David and Goliath

That this gamine matador
Should stop the bull of Winter
Is nothing short of amazing
Gored by the picadors of the early sun
He is merely enraged
But he is no match for the snowdrop
With his braids of aconite
And his cape of moonlight
The sword
When it finally falls
Feels more like a knighthood
It is almost an honour
To plunge into the dust
Before such precocity
The snowdrop takes a bow
And leaves the arena
Which is already being cleared
For the new season.

Galapagos Finches

Similar finches with different beaks
Gave Darwin pause for sea-sick weeks
As he retched in his cabin
And pondered nightly
Over common birds
With different tools
For nicking nectar
From flowery hooves
Some with nutcrackers
Some with spoons
Some with chisels
And some with brooms
Each of them evolved
To fit the bill
Of the empty niche
They had flown to fill.

Note on poem: Although it is now generally recognized that it was the Mockingbirds rather than the finches of the Galapagos which were instrumental in formulating Darwin's idea of Natural Selection and these some time after his return from his global journey it is the finches he also collected which most people now recognize as being emblematic of his theory and their iconic status has been enhanced in recent years by a long term study of the birds which shows the principles of Natural Selection operating in real time and although many now think that it was his earlier discoveries of fossilized giant tree sloth's and armadillos on the coast of Argentina that first began fermenting his overarching theory it is the finches that have lodged themselves in the popular imagination.

For those wishing to study the subject in greater depth 'The Beak of the Finch' - the modern classic which charts the most recent study of the Galapagos Finches is highly recommended.

Ostriches

Mata Hari's on drumstick legs
With beautiful lashes
And boxing glove feet
Ostriches carry their beautiful tresses
Bouncing above the can-canning heat
Bearing their thighs for all to see
Plenty of African flightless meat
Plenty of flounces and plenty of curves
And beautiful plush on their Moulin Rouge seats.

King of the Lewis Hoard

I sit in a chair
Carved from silence
Sensing the chequerboard of nights and waves
On which my sea lord's long ship sways
Ferried in a box from the Golden Horn
Inlaid with the pearl of the unicorn
I am part of Tostig's precious navy
A Viking sea lord of the mind
Amongst the hold I bump and grind
With Freya here - my precious queen
The Morningstar of Tostig's dreams
He saw a box from Samarkand
So loved the game he tried his hand
And had this chess set carved himself
Reflecting all his plundered wealth
We are the Gods of mortal men
The pantheon that succours them
But over there - across the sea
Are other Gods that menace me
The chief of these is Christ the King
Whose bishops - waiting in the wings
Are planning to outflank my pawns
With promise of a life re-born
But whilst I sail the seven realms
With Thor and Loki at the helm
I will not fear his wooden cross
The raging fires of Ragnarok
I will not be baptized with water
For valour only comes with slaughter
Valhalla will assign my fate
The Fisherman may reach my gates
But then I will unleash my knights
My sea wolves of the Northern Lights
And in a brave and dreadful fight
Will slaughter all these brides of Christ
Valhalla will assign my fate
Then Tostig say to Christ "Checkmate."

Note on poem. Long ago a herdsman on the shores of Lewis in the Outer Hebrides killed a survivor from a shipwreck for the bundle he was carrying. It contained a heap of menacing little carved images. Convinced that they were the sailor's Gods the frightened killer buried them.

Years later he confessed, when about to be hanged for another murder, but his prudent listeners decided to let sleeping Gods lie. It was not until 1831 that a crofter re-discovered them. When sent for sale they were recognized as ancient chessmen and are now acclaimed as one of our greatest and most enigmatic treasures.

The pieces, exquisitely carved from walrus ivory now reside in the British Museum and in Edinburgh.

Chess has always been a battle of opposing forces and in this poem I line the ancient Gods of the Norse world against the encroaching God of Christianity. Christ of course was the victor for, in the end The Vikings saw many similarities between this redemptive figure and their own God Odin, hanged on the World Tree... But the battle was long.

Folklore Myths and Legends of Britain.

Manta Ray

Long before Star Wars and Stealth bombers
I was tucked up in bed
With the autobiography of Hans Hass
Diving to adventure with the Manta Ray
This was the Close Encounter I dreamed of
There was nothing more alien than this
Nothing more awesome than the vast
Undulations of Neptune's outrider.
It was the deeps atavistic pterodactyl
Part of the Nazgul's submarine contingent
And I was its secret pilot
Coming in low over the coral
On the supple diamond
Black as Mecca
To drop the fires of my imagination
On a sea floor lit by a bedside light.

Note on poem: Hans Hass was one of my childhood heroes; a name to conjure with before the arrival of Jacques Cousteau and his ilk. Originally he earned his living by spearing the creatures he later came to love and admire. His two best known books are 'Under the Red Sea' and 'Diving to Adventure' which are still well worth reading.
Manta Rays remain one of my favourite creatures and I would love to swim amongst them one day..!

Premature Epiphany: *For George*

Here - in the swaddling clothes of the New Year
He told me about their new baby
The first snowdrop
Pallid - frail - scare half made up
Germinating in a glass uterus
A 21st century manger.
He was born in a flood of Christmas blood
But survived
Thanks to 3 gifts
The Myrrh of medicine
The Gold of technology
And
Most precious of all
The Frankincense of a Mother's love.

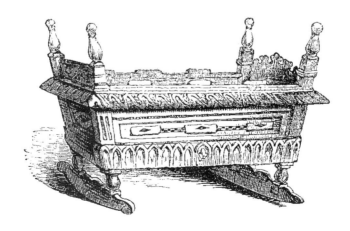

Solstice Sunday

Bat on willow
Village clock
Scent of tea
And key in lock
Sandwiches sliced nice and thin
Steeple's shadow
Lengthening…
Peal of bells and scent of hay
11 played and won the day
Then to the pub for ale and cheer
On this
The turning of the year.

Penguins

Penguins enjoy listening to the music of waltzing icebergs
Penguins enjoy balancing their Penguiny eggs on their yellowy legs
Penguins enjoy standing under the Albert Hall
Of the Aurora Borealis
Watching Orion conduct the Penguin Suite
Penguins enjoy snow operas and ice cream sodas
Penguins enjoy sliding about on their bottoms
Like brakeless Skodas
But - most of all Penguins like to
Fly underwater…
Free-falling off the ice cliffs
Like newspaper Lemmings
They open their stubby throttles
Like formerly sedate - opera going Flemings
Then roar into swanhood
Blasting off into the icicled Antarctic
Hitting Top C
Leaving a lot of surprised people with empty wrappers
Feeling deeply embarrassed that they'd made fun of these
Blubbery - snow vested Pavarottis
These black and white chocolaty flappers
That were meant for their afternoon tea.

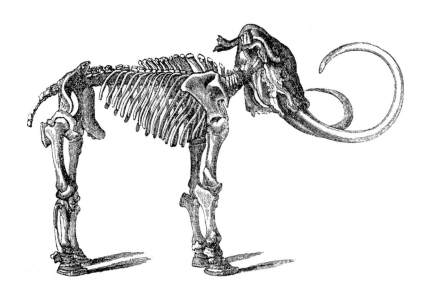

Pleistocene Sky

See above you
The Constellation of the Mammoth…?
The starlit horns of the Auroch
The fiery antlers of the Irish Elk
Follow the path
Of the shining water…
See the salmon
Leaping through moonlit milk…?
Now watch the star man stalk his prey
And bless the spear you made today.

Vultures

Vultures are Africa's rag and bone men
Dustbin birds employed by house-proud nature
To vacuum the savannah clean of offal
With their cockney neckerchiefs
And their bony smiles
They ride the hot whirlpools of African air
For hundreds of hopeful African miles
Gimlet eyes ghosting for ghastly gristle

Then
Clumping down in their undertaker's robes
Like a squadron of intemperate flying toads
They squabble rudely by the meat kitchen door
Till the lions can gorge themselves no more

Three hours later
The zebra is clean as a whistle
And they are circling once again
A storm of leathery - foetid epistles
With their weather eyes cocked
On the next main chance
Like Baron Von Richthofen
Hovering over France…

Celtic Wheel

January
Cairngorm Evening

The moon
Resting in the antlers
Of the red deer.

February
Perfunctory

If that was a kiss
So is dew
Melting on a lonely man.

March
Before the dance

Within the chrysalis of the bulb
The daffodil
Arranges her crinoline.

April

A dream of bluebells
Reminds me of lapis lazuli
The girl with the Nile
In her palm-swept eyes.

May
Surprised by Joy

After Winter's pregnant pause
The cherry blossoms
Pink applause.

June
Mouth of Lugh

Erected on the solstice path
These sarsen lips
Sip Summer's draught.

July

Searching for the answer to crop circles
Round and round
The scarecrow.

August

A wasp
Banging on my bamboo blind
Millimetres from an open window.

September
For Paddy 1984 –1998

After 14 years
The cat-flap still
The Autumn moon on the empty garden.

October
A Glass for Compo

Feeling sorry for the Autumn scarecrow
I gave him the last
Of the Summer wine.

November
Owl

He hoots beneath the silver moon
His feathers shine like gold doubloons
He floats across the evening sky
A dark - avenging lullaby.

December

The fir cone opens its shutters
Like a breathing pagoda
Snaps them shut in the crystal wind.

Saharan Crocodiles: *For Walter Miller Jr*
Author of A Canticle for Leibowitz

Here
In the midst of barchans
The sands that buried a sphinx
Time
And time again
Is a secret oasis
Lagoon of the lotus flower…
Shade your eyes from the glare
Peer beneath the overhang
And
There…
Can you see them…?
Egypt's living reliquaries
The lost menagerie of Ozymandias
The remnant of that fossilized religion
That built stone spaceships
And golden time machines
In a vain attempt to outwit time
Ozymandias has long since toppled into the sands
But here - in this lost sanctuary to Sobek
The Saharan crocodiles continue to bask
And when we - all that we are and all that we have been
Have followed the road to dusty death
And our skyscrapers point from glaciers
Here
In the midst of barchans
The sands that buried Cairo
Time and time again
The crocodiles will continue…

*Note on Poem: Sobek was the Egyptian crocodile God.
Walter Miller Jr is famous for the post-apocalyptic novel of the
title. The Saharan crocodiles were only discovered a few
years ago. They had survived in their secret redoubt for the
last 4000 years in what was once a verdant land.*

Look... at the Snow...!

Today I took time out
Just to unwind
The snow came down
After bright sunlight
Moving in strange combinations
Apart from a few runners
I had the World to myself
Look I tried to say to them
Look... at the snow...!
But of course
No one was listening
They just stared at me
As they ran past
Thinking
Who is that mad bugger
Whispering...?

Floral Dance

The flowers in cadence come and go
Like wavebands on a radio
Like chorus dancers in a show
Like actors in a wooden O
Where each one has the chance to shine
Upon the spinning Globe of time
Where each one is a sun-drenched prop
In Shakespeare's magic lantern box
Which has its hour upon the stage
Its name in lights on Nature's page
Which plays its part in Arden's glades
Then curtseys as it slowly fades
The glories of its fancy dress
All bound in memories flower press.

Snails

Wandering homewards after Summer rain
I have often found snails
Fully rigged on their silver seas
Leaving the ports of lamp-lit gardens
And I have stooped down
Like some fastidious Jain
Again
    and again
        and again
            and again
To plant them back in the comfort of gardens
Safe from the anvils of moon-cracking thrushes
The churning wheels of brightly lit buses
And the crunching heels of unthinking lovers
Too busy fanning each other's ardour
And too busy smoothing each other's pain
To notice the shipwreck of chestnut Armadas
Wandering homeless after Summer rain.

A Poem for Andy Goldsworthy

Look…!
Here is a man
Working with light
Explaining Creation in Nature's classroom
Here is our Basho with wind chaffened hands
Pointing the way to the suchness of seasons
Here is a shepherd with a sutra in his heart
Show casing nature with frost-riven art
And here is a shaman who lives in the seasons
Here is a poet who dresses in leaves
Like a marvellous scarecrow
Who blesses the birds
Who coaxes them down from the wintery trees
Then climbs from his cross
When no one is looking
To polish the stars on his snow-sprinkled sleeves.

184

Sheepdog: *For Phil Drabble*

A four legged field radio
A scampering chess-board
Alert to every whistling nuance
The sheep-shadower
Slouches and sleuths
On invisible strings of obedience
Dancing to the skylark of a man's fluted fingers
And the sheep are nudged by waves of fear
Bolstering together in exact increments of terror
As the sheepdog quivers at the edge of instinct
Balanced on the razor between hunt and herd
Poised at the still point of the rustling heather.

Celtic Vows

1

Handfast: *Maddy's Meadow - May 1998. For Linda*

I give this circle of the sun
To symbolize that we are one
I take the star down from the sky
To circle round your Irish eyes
And then I place it on your hand
Transmuted to a wedding band
Whilst you now do the same for me
The green earth mixing with the sea.

2

Celtic Wedding Wheel
Maddy's Meadow - May 1998. For Linda

We meet within this wheel of trees
To bind each other by degrees
Wild flowers at Stations of the Sun
Protect us from the harmful ones
Whilst birdsong forms a sacred shower
That cloaks us with its joyful power
As - stitched into the web of life
The Green Man clasps his Beltane wife.

Mole

Deep beneath the furrowed land
The blind skin-opener
With his wicket-keeping hands
Is scrabbling through Stygian gloom
Like a venerable scholar
In a star-less room
Wading through his Stilton
With a port-stained spoon.

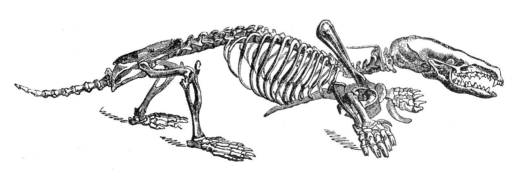

Llama 'Kaaarrma'...!

I once asked in Lima a Llama
What he thought of the doctrine of Karma...?
He replied that he once preached
In snow-capped Tibet
So poor spelling was something
He'd always regret.

Misplaced: *For W.B. Yeats*

The life that we might once have led
Is pictured here
Inside my head
The walks - the talks - the passions felt
The memories shared upon the shelf
A life lived with a kindred soul
A jeu d'esprit of mingled goals
Of meetings kept and trysts maintained
Of Eros dancing in the rain
A sense of rightness duly felt
The certitude of Commonwealth
The knotwork of a Celtic cross
Combining both our joy and loss
A torc of twisted golden steel
The clay thrown on a common wheel
A hedge enclosing common ground
A barrow on a mist-swept down
In which two skeletons embrace
And share the same eternal space
As high above a yew tree grows
And round about a river flows
The verities of love and death
All dance in hope's eternal dress
And look back at what might have been
A drover's track of broken dreams
The woman with the shattered jar
The Jokerman with his guitar
And all the lyrics of my life
Interred with someone else's wife.

Mills & Boon Times Two

1

Barbara Cartland's Cherry Blossom Dream
For Colin Firth

Barbara Cartland's dream of snow
All décolletage
And chintzy bows
A chesterfield of candied flocks
On which to strew her blue-rinsed locks
And write of heroes dark and bold
Her D'Arcy's well hung centrefolds
Her damsels quivering jelly moulds
Marshmallows melting in the sun
Coy Debutantes with nothing on.

2

Barbara Cartland's Flamingo

The Flamingo is so very pink
She blushes when she stoops to drink
She's Barbara Cartland's favourite bird
That mistress of the rose-bud word
And when she flies into the sun
The colours of her wing tips run
To paint a soft carnation dusk
That's filled with sugar-coated lust.

Schools out for Summer: *Bradgate Park, Leicestershire*

They bring the children they once were
To celebrate this lovely place
Where deer browse under leaf-limbed space
And squirrels run their Summer race
The plastic charms of city life
Are vapid
And will not suffice
For we have never quite outgrown
The woods we call our second home
And need to walk in dappled space
To feel the healing hand of grace.

Note on Poem: Bradgate Park in Leicestershire was formerly the seat of the Greys and the ruins of Lady Jane Grey's majestic Elizabethan house stand surrounded by strutting peacocks and the beautiful deer park. It is said that, after Lady Jane Grey's execution all the oaks in the park on the road leading to the house were beheaded as a mark of respect and there are certainly many strangely stunted and twisted oaks to be found on the avenue leading to the house. The park sprawls across the slopes of an extinct Cambrian volcano and is covered in bracken and stone-walled copses. It was given to the people of Leicestershire for the rest of time by the last owner and has provided great solace, comfort and joy for the people of Leicestershire ever since.

Ninety Niner

In his mother's oven
The ninety niner bakes
Soaked in malted vinegar
Marbled through with hate
For nothing's ever cracked
The old contender's skin
His hide is stegasaurian
Fiercely boiled in vim
His atoms packed together
Like sardines in a tin
And woe betide the oner
Who aims to chance his luck
In clashing with this 'conkeror'
Whose hundredth scalp looms up.

Penny for the Guy: *For Victor Meldrew and Randy Newman*

Towards the end of October
Children stand on street corners
Asking for money to burn their Grandfathers
This is a peculiarly British institution
Nowhere else in the world
Is such a bizarre form of euthanasia practised
But Grandfathers are a burden
A species beyond *our Ken*
Who go on and on about the Second World War
And how the world was so much better then
And this seems as good a method as any
Of ridding the world of such redundant men
And a lot less protracted than the earlier method
Of hanging - drawing and quartering them.

Leatherback Turtle

She has been crying for millions of years

This beautiful pea-green boat
This upturned coracle of sadness

For millions of tears
Evolution has sucked her back

Out of the blue dress of the sea
And onto the sands of indignity

To lay the eggs that will - in time
Reprise this mournful pantomime

As clockwork toys whirr out to sea
To start new turtle families.

Wren: *For D.H. Lawrence*

A tiny match box dinosaur
The hedgerow's chintzy Minotaur
We view this thimbleful of bones
From safety in our windowed homes
But if we'd met him in the park
Before the sailing of the ark
He would be taller than the trees
And we'd be trying not to sneeze.

A Blustery day at The British Open, Royal Birkdale 2008
For Peter Allis

Amidst the wild and windy spray
The ball is tempest-tossed today
A hostage to the gales that blow
And buffet all the raucous crows
Spectators of the highs and lows
Played out upon the links below
Where all the amateurs and pros
Are caught up in the ebb and flow
Of drive and chip and wedge and putt
And "Oh... That isn't good enough...!"
Of "Four!" and "Shot!" and "Oh... well played...!"
For everyone has Tiger days
All wryly voiced by Peter Allis
The doyen of life's golfing chalice
With parables for Everyman
Who slices through the promised land
Reminding us it's just a game
Of joy and sorrow - sun and rain
Of ifs and buts and might have beens
Of highs and lows - old claret dreams
All rounded off by magic scenes
Played out upon life's putting greens.

Song of Taliesin

I shape-shift into Autumn trees
And mourn the waning of their leaves

I glide upon the seventh wave
A salmon leaping to its grave

I as an eagle circle high
Inspect the realms in which I fly

I as a stag ascend the moor
And bellow from a mist wrapped tor

I as a stone uphold the sky
A menhir till the day I die

I as a shaman enter in
I am the shape of everything.

196

The Leaning Tower of Pisa

The Viagra of many minds
Has failed to halt its sharp decline

Once proud - erect and Heaven sent
This campanile is frankly bent

This tipsy marble wedding cake
For centuries has not been straight

And cannot probe the stratosphere
Because it's declinations queer

This lovely marble clad giraffe
This penis flying at half mast

Is Casanova past his peak
Unsteady on his gouty feet

Inclining like a chocolate flake
That's sinking in an ice cream lake

Yet no one wants the flaccid tower
To regain all its primal power

A tower of Pisa fully straight
Would not bring people through the gates

Just like the Mona Lisa's smile
They like its enigmatic style

It shows that wily city states
Can make the proudest of mistakes

That building upon shifting sands
Undoes the work of many hands

The only chance of lightning's grace
Is built upon the rock of faith

Which binds our towers with trusting glue
Ensuring that our aim is true.

197

And it was all Yellow: *Or Richard Jefferie's Lament*

Our land is parcelled out to rape
It's beauty is a vast mistake
Where once the wild flower knitted in
Hegemony of beef is king
Where once the skylark lit the dawn
There's nothing now but marching corn
No longer ruled by Nature's clock
Monotony has run amok
And where the hedgerows stitched the land
Like veins inside the Green Man's hand
There's nothing on this sterile sea
As far as you or I can see.

Swallow Tales

1

Swallows compose Summer's elegy
As they decorate singing telegraph wires
With crotchety feathered cadenzas

They are leaving for Africa
A skein of Elgar
A flock of Greensleeves
Seeding Worcestershire in Ngorongoro

Upon their return
Something of Africa
Will bloom in the breasts of the Malverns
Then Bill Hedgebutts will write in to Gardener's Question Time
To ask what he can do
About Warthogs rooting up brassicas
Thomson's gazelle nibbling window cake
And elephants sitting in wheelbarrows.

2

An arrow from his bow of wings
The swallow through the Summer
Swings
Then swivels on his Autumn arc
And hurtles past the dreaming lark
Eloping through the falling leaves
A skimming stone on darkling seas.

Goshawk: *For T.H. White*

A captive cloud leopard
Clasped on the wrist
Like a dark knight that dreams
In the shield feathered lists
This slip-streamed crossbow
Of high towered elms
Twists and burns in his moon-blinkered helm
Then
Flowers above our sun-leavened Kingdom
To hammer the quarry
In his blood sprinkled realm
Returning again
Like a faithful retainer
Spiralling down to the grain quilted floor
To land again on the wrist of the aimer
Who unleashed this dawn-dappled
Minion of war.

Note on Poem: Although T.H. White is, of course best known for his marvellous Arthurian Fantasy of a Mediaeval world that never was, although it should have been.!
He was also an excellent writer on nature in general and The Goshawk, his account of his attempt to train the bird of the poem's title is a little classic of its own and explains the great knowledge of falconry to be found in 'The Sword in the Stone'.

Shiva's Love Song: *For W.H. Auden and ?*

Start all the clocks
Unzip the moon
Release a cloud of red balloons
Start all the clocks
Unpack the sun
Abandon sadness
Feeling glum
I am no longer on my own
The dog has found a brand new bone
She is my morning - noon and night
The compass points of my delight
She is my angel of the East
Her train a skein of snow white geese
'The Wind's Twelve Quarters' I have found
My princess from a golden town
So everything will now get better
Like rainbows after stormy weather
And I am floating like a kite
Upon the wings of my delight.

Winter Rainbow: *Cathedral Close, Norwich*

Cycling to work on a crisp Winter day
Beneath this rainbow's prismatic gleam
I watch God with his outstretched cosmic scarf
Supporting his favourite local team.

Stonehenge

Here is a circle made of stones
A great quern for the solar throne
Which ground the semen of the sun
Baked golden loaves for everyone

Here are the doorways to the sun
Vaginas for the horned one
Who spills his seed on Summer's day
In Winter's postern bleeds away

Here is a Catherine wheel of winds
Apollo's megalithic crown
The womb in which the stars were forged
And every season melted down

And here is a doorway out of time
The still point of this turning rhyme
Where - at the centre of the stones
A shaman danced among the bones.

Bonfire Night

A tapestry of burning lights
Is spread above the clouds tonight

A magic carpet made of fire
A Golden Fleece of twisted fire

For this is Autumn's masque of Spring
A mirage borne on smoking wings

That covers Earth from North to South
With flames poured from a dragon's mouth.

Archaeopteryx: *For Claire*

Smash open the Book of Time
And Archaeopteryx is dancing
Throwing out limbs of feathered limestone
Printed by lithographic silts
It is flying across the pediment of history
Pressed - like a stone flower
A jigsaw of tempered porcelain
It is an Elgin marble
A Magellan of air
Daedalus by Da Vinci
A Harpy floating on a vase of sculptured clouds.

THE FIRST KNOWN LAND BIRD

A Poem for Flidais: *Irish Goddess of the woods*

I am the Goddess of the woods
A spirit seldom understood

Great Herne the Hunter is my groom
He rules the Sun - I rule the Moon

And when the sun shines on the land
He takes me by my milk white hand

And leads me up the woodland path
To make green love upon the grass

And when the waves break on the sand
He gives to me a Celtic band

A ring that's made of emerald stones
He found within a hill of bones

And when the snow lies on the path
We gather round the sacred hearth

To pluck love from the dulcet harp
And bless the New Year's pulsing heart.

Gethsemane Cockerel

I was the cock who crowed at two
When Peter said
I know not you..!

I was the cock who crowed at three
When Peter said
I am not me....!

I was the cock who crowed no more
When Peter wept
And truly saw

I was the cock at Heaven's door
When God went to the threshing floor.

How the Robin Became

The dowdy bird at Christmas sings
A canticle on snow flake wings
For - flying past the Magi's star
He found the cradled Avatar
And sang a song on Mary's lawn
A Rubaiyat to wake the dawn

The rosehip bird at Easter brims
A chalice borne on Angel's wings
For - flying past the Saviour's cross
His breast was sprayed with scarlet drops
And now he sings on Easter morn
Resplendent from a crown of thorns.

207

A Haikuesque Yearbook

January
Mammoth Meditation

Siberius standing for snow-swept hours
Lost in a meadow
Of Pleistocene flowers.

February
For Mary Webb

The first bee
Mils the last snowdrop
Of Winter honey.

March

The crocuses have punched the clock
And flounced out in their saffron frocks
To shine like gas jets in the rain
A wind blown Amish counterpane.

April
Yellow Laugh

The daffodils
Leap out from the brown palette
Of Autumn's remains
Like a shout of joy
In a Gentleman's Club.

May

Young geisha's look up
With cherry blossom faces
The sun dawns
Through their laughing fingers.

June

Climbing Uffington vale
A skylarks bright alarum
Drifts across this empty hill.

July
Still Life: *For Maria Guerten*
Painter and tile maker
Died Norwich, Summer 1998

The studio laid out
Just as she left it
Get Well flowers still blooming.

August
Wet Dream

All day the man rests inside her
Like a rock pool
Left by passing waves.

September
Orion

Look…!
Low in the Autumn sky
A glow worm on the hawthorn.

October
Grendel

Marsh flaring eyes
Dripping into the Dark Ages
With a six pack of men.

November

Flaring from my sparkler
Ephemeral constellations.

December
Haiku for a Robin

In my emptied garden
This glass of Autumn wine
Brims on Winter's table.

Girl with a Pearl Earring: *Portrait by Vermeer*

The smile slips from her painted lips
As she watches you across the lounge

A charming girl from a small Dutch town
Whose eyes still follow you around

As if to say "When can we meet...?
I shan't be long... I'll be discreet...!

When Vermeer's gone we'll paint the town...

Just hand me down
Just hand me down...

Then walk with me..
Through my charming town..."

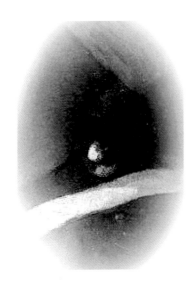

Transition

Wheeling like escaping leaves
The geese sweep over sleeping trees

Their destination is the sun
That shines beyond the fowler's gun

And as they flicker overhead
The Green Man turns his burning head

To watch the Summer passing by
As comets light the geese filled sky.

The flutes of Autumn fly at dawn
When Herne the hunter
Blows his horn.

Norfolk Fly - Past

Against the splendour of a Cotman sky
The brush-stroked geese go floating by

And as their skeins bank overhead
The marsh below is flooded red

And as they swing towards the sun
The fowler points his loaded gun

To scatter flocks like hand-tossed grain
Dissolving into Autumn rain.

River Creatures

I am the heron
Praying for fish

On the plate of the moon
My twinkling dish

I am the stickleback of English streams
A silver comb from a mermaid's dream

I am the pike who skulks alone
A cutlass from a broken home

I am the kingfisher soaring high
Oberon's jewel in the Winter sky.

Samhain at Sutton Hoo

1

The Earth - now weather - beaten gold
Has turned to face the haunting cold
The armour of the ancient knight
Is rusting in the weeping light
The oak has lost his Summer crown
The birch mislaid her greengage gown
As in amongst the mist-wreathed mounds
The grave-robbed spirits
Flicker round…

Owl's Saga

2

Tu-Whit Tu-Whoo - at Sutton Hoo
A king lies near his motley crew
A sliver surfer sleeping proud
Beneath the scudding Suffolk clouds
The white-caps of a Winter sky
Which broach the mounds where sailor's lie
And drive a fleet of buried men
To Ragnarok and back again
From there to sail into the West
And reach the mead halls of the blessed.

213

Kingfisher: *The Washbrook, Knighton Park, Leicester*

Gone before you've seen him
The brain only catches up
With the afterburners
The hummingbird glimmer
Of the jump-jet javelin
The incandescent Inca
The shimmering pocket rocket
The fastest cast on the Washbrook
The Back to the Future bird
The Mission Impossible marvel
With his surcoat of streaming pearls.

Not a Kingfisher: *For Magritte*

Wrought in all mediums
Metal - oil and watercolours
He outflashes them all
Picks all artistic locks
Slip-stitches the Autumn water
Slips through the finest net
Of our finest imaginings
And burns away across an evening river.

Kingfisher's Ring

Bird of the turning earth
Covered in ocean and land
You are the birth stone of Gaia
Worn on her moon-dancing hand.

Standard Romance

We split up on bonfire night…
I lit the green touch-paper of jealousy
And she disappeared
Trailing her flaming pearls…

In the morning
Raking over the ashes
I found the Black Box of our life

Then I tracked her for weeks in another's gravity
Followed the flight path of my rocket girl

Until I found her in a crater with a rocket man
Caught her 'in flagrante' with a passing Martian

And monitored her landing on a distant world.

Roe Deer

Amongst the forest saplings moved
Small dappled trees with cloven hooves
They shifted in the fading light
Their gilded haunches poised for flight
And then they washed across the glade
And as they dried began to fade
Their forms receding up the glen
And melting round the twilight Ben.

Deer in Earlham Road Cemetery...?

It was Bruce who told me there were deer in the cemetery
Hidden under small trees
Blooming at dusk
Somehow they had seeped through railings
Painted themselves in with a velvety brush
To leave on the air
In the dew of the morning
A faint efflorescence
Like sweet spirits laughing
The scent of their passing
The lawns tinged with musk.

The Legionnaire's Tale
A lost Chaucerian Fragment

"We cast some lots to take the Robe
A roll of dice for Treasure Trove
I folded up the caul of God
And with the legions miles I trod...

I lost it in a tavern brawl
Some gladiator took the shawl...

I've searched for it in many shrines
Purporting to have Holy finds
Through many lands and many times...

And then for Turin did I make
To castigate the final fake.
Yet - when the casque was there undone
I saw the Robe that I had won
The very fleece was there unfurled
That cloaked the Saviour of the World
And on it was the thorn-scratched face
That welcomed me to Heaven's Gate."

Old Flame

"I still want a baby" she said
"It might not be too late..."

And the years passed by like empty wombs
All her men just doors into empty rooms

I could not help - I looked away
For once I was her man they say

Yes - once I was a swinging door
A man who left her years before

Who could have helped conceive a child
To light bare rooms undomiciled.

Thoughts on the Thought Fox: *For Ted Hughes*

The fox has left the bookshop shelves
The traps been sprung by we ourselves
For art is under lock and key
But all can shoplift poetry
So everyone who drinks the potion
Can keep the thought fox as a totem
He lives inside as many heads
As scan the snow he softly treads
This poem may be a National Treasure
But everyone can poach its pleasure
His foxiness is there to find
He waits to enter every mind
Created out of ink and paper
His world is there for every taker
And therein lies the wealth of words
More priceless than a poacher's birds
That midnight moment on the page
Which will endure from age to age
Wherever those who read and write
Can scan the forests of the night
And watch the thought fox boldly come
When snow and ink and brain are one.

Glastonbury Carp

Older then the pool is old
Solder laced with scales of gold
Covered in the verdigris
Accrued throughout the centuries
The carp lies many fathoms deep
A sunset caught in carved relief
The wisest thing within the mere
The breastplate laid on Arthur's bier.

Evening Carp

We sat at the head of the lake
And watched the great carp roll
In the lengthening evening
Splashing in the sunset of our glasses.

Sam Gamgee's Carp

His scales are tiles from elven halls
The leaves of Mallorn in the Fall
His coat of Mithril's finely wrought
Embossed with gold from Gondor's court
The sunfish of freshwater streams
The evening's last refulgent gleam
He slips behind the misty peaks
Of Minas Tirith - wreathed in sleep.

If we could live and be as trees: *For W.H. Davies*

If we could live and be as trees
We'd measure time in centuries
And have more time to feel the air
The seasons passing through our hair
If we could live and be as trees
We'd have more time to stand and stare
If we could grow through light and air
We'd see the Green Man smiling there.

Sunset Dragonfly

Here he comes
Whirling from the prehistoric
Graduating from the soup kitchens
Of Summer streams
With his honeycomb goggles
And his soap-bubble wings
Da Vinci's swirling rotor blades
Emerging from the Autumn haze
An ash seed - spinning in the dusk
A bow tie flecked with wanderlust.

Sycamore Seeds

Sycamore seeds are fallopian tubes
Beautiful X-rays of trees in the nude

Sycamore seeds are earrings of light
Delicate wing-nuts that turn in the light

Sycamore seeds are dragonfly husks
Dryads of Summer that spin in the dusk

And sycamore seeds are the keys on the ring
Of the door of the seasons

That opens on Spring.

The Oxymoron

The Oxymoron hunts by night
But - sad to say he's not that bright
And sometimes hunts himself by day
And kills himself in the affray.

Starlings at Samhain

Smoke signals forming in the shamanic sky
Miasmic murmurations in the blink of an eye
A close encounter with the mother ship
The Shadowmancer flashing his bag of tricks
A starfish - an eagle - a comet - a whale
Don Quixote jousting with a windmill's sails
A baitball of herring - a geisha's fan
Agincourt's arrows arching overland
The flick of a switch - the blink of an eye
A prayer flag streaming in a snow leopard sky
A jellyfish pulsing - an algal bloom
A lunar model landing on a Thanksgiving moon
The genie emerging from Aladdin's lamp
The bath plug pulled on a Northern bank
The Piper of Hamelin with rats on his tail
The chaff thrown up by an Autumn flail
The Nazgul swirling round Sauron's ring
A city of angels on the head of a pin
Ectoplasm dancing for Conan Doyle
A King Cobra rising from his Sanskrit coils
A twister approaching a Kansas shack
The Dam Busters flying through tracer and flack
The blink of an eye - the flick of a switch
The bonfire night ride of a cackling witch
Niagran descent of a fire breathing flock
The lid slammed shut on the shape-shifter's box.

A North American Indian explains Systems Theory
For Hugh Brody

Know that the land is a web and a flow
Know that nothing is greater
Man is of a piece with the beaver - the elk and the cedar
In felling the cedar a seed is planted
In killing the elk prayers are offered
In killing the beaver room and time is left for others to grow

In the land of web and flow man treads the path
And leaves no trace
Neither high nor low man is himself the ebb and flow
Through the flowing land ebbs the hunter
Through the web of the spider the seasons come and go

No webs are broken here

In the forest the flowing hunter follows the Tao
And everything rejoices in relation.

Emperors, take 2: *A second glance at For Pam*

Thermos flasks in serried ranks
Centurions in frozen pants
Sherbet fountains dipped in yolk
Orchids wrapped in duffel coats
Candles made of blubber wax
Pavarottis sent by fax
A field of Elvis Presley clones
With 'love me tender' mobile phones
A plain of frosty walnut whips
Of Pickwicks on dyspeptic trips
Van Morrison's in veedon fleece
All wrapped in thought for astral weeks
A coach of obese Charlie Chaplins
Waddling on the beach at Maplins
A love in at an oyster stall
A fat clubs massive Winter ball
A Gulag Archipelago
Of sumo wrestlers in the snow
Inured to Winter's scything pain
Their giant egg a ball and chain
They wait for months - like New Age men
A brood of glacial father hens
Beneath the glowing Southern lights
They soldier on like men in tights
Until their fishwives - lost at sea
Return to claim their mini me's
And let their freezing daddies go
To fish amongst the melting snow
And put on all the pounds mislaid
Through all those 'pregnant' phantom days
With cod and chips and mushy peas
Washed down with Stella Artois seas.

227

Still-born graves - Earlham Road Cemetery, Norwich

A secluded area of the cemetery the graves rife with balloons, teddy bears, windmills and Disney characters.

This is the fairground that never was
This is the fairground that never began
For here lie the playmates of Peter Pan
The Never Ever children from Never Never land.

Zooplankton

Across the vast unbounded sea
Cavorts a whole menagerie
A science fiction omnibus
That's filled with harpoons - flails and tusks
A smorgasboard of melting snow
That churns with nightmares from below
Just when you thought the ark was full
Here comes another tentacle
A triple sided palindrome
A sea squirt with a mobile phone
There's more to life than meets the eye
Phantasmagoric bubbleflies
A vast paella of the weird
The beautiful
The strange
The feared
A gallimaufry of the sea
A bestiary on L.S.D.
But don't have nightmares
Most are small
And cannot eat you up at all
No - don't have nightmares
Do sleep tight
Your bed is Noah's Ark tonight
Beneath your headboard dolphins swim
On lovely starlit dolphin fins
Whilst all around you
Out to sea
The waters glow with mystery.

Not Love... actually

Not

I fancy her
She fancies NOT
She fancies me
I fancy NOT
And so the world keeps spinning round
With no one finding common ground
Except for NOT who all agree
Is everybody's cup of tea.

Blue Suede Stratocaster

I loved your rock and roll behind
It's denim covered bluish rind
But now those curves are left behind
Your bum notes wobble through my mind.

On the Contrary...We regretted Everything

We had a café au lait
Spent a vile day near the Champs Elysées
You were angry
I was sad
The Eiffel tower was raving mad
We should have come for le weekend
Before we both went round the bend
We should have come before as friends
Paris is for starts...not ends.

We Carved our Names

We carved our names into the tree
And hemmed them with a moated heart
But as the tree grew rings of fate
The mildewed names were drawn apart
And now a moat divides our lives
Incised upon that Summer pine
And nothing stops the widening sea
The Continental Drift of time.

No Luck at M&S

I gave you love
You gave it back
It hadn't even been unpacked
I took it back - but can't exchange
It's unrequited

What a shame...

Gannets

They dive
Like Acapulco men
Beneath the waves
And up again
They learn to plunge
In silent streams
A flock of falling guillotines
White Stukas of the evening air
They dive bomb with unerring flair
A rain of arrows from the fold
To strafe the oceans cloth of gold
Returning to the evening sky
With gobbets of stargazey pie
Wild pirates of the azure foam
All Neptune's archers flying home.

Puffin

Clown of the Orkney's
Lear's fool to the Fastnett wind
Bobbin of beautiful water
More fish than fowl
Monogamous as the owl
Wearing his medals in his technicolour beak
Sand eels dredged from the Northern deeps
Then hung like washing on a line
A shuttlecock trawler
In the summertime.

231

The Fritillary Fairy: *For Cicely Mary Baker*

You are the bulb that shines for me
The purple crowned fritillary
The elves hat on a slender stalk
That lights the path on which I walk
You are the being who warms my hearth
Titania with the silver laugh
And when I saw you first I knew
That love was purple through and through
And then you kissed me and I knew
That flowers could be fairies too.

Rook

The rook
Has a black intelligence
An avian Hells' Angel
He loves his tribe
For he is the biker
Of the Autumn skies
And he knows scarecrows
Are straw filled men
He skewers their eyes
To feed his ken
And lives aloft
In the rookery wood
In a nest of chapters
Oozing blood
And caws aloft at the biker's hub
In a raucous - querulous Hell Fire Club.

Autumn Blackbird

A muezzin of dusk and dawn
His pulpit is the wind blown thorn
From which he preaches
Night and day
The glories of the rightful way
He ushers in the honeyed sun
And then - when vespers have begun
He brings to us the roundy moon
An apple on his dunking spoon
A lantern in the Northern sky
To light his leaf-swept lullaby.

New Walk Transfigured: *Leicester, Autumn 2006*
For Thomas Traherne

I walked down avenues of gold
The love letters of time grown old
A ticker tape of falling leaves
Glissanding from the Autumn trees
A threnody of whispered rain
All gusting down the wind blown lane
A glossary of golden snow
Alighting on the leaves below
And gilding earth with golden leaf
Illuminating Gospel streets
The very shards of shattered glass
The diadems in Heaven's mask
The Book of Kells beneath my seat
The mellow mists that captured Keats
The people all immortal wheat
The bread presented by the priest
The shining host of Autumn sheaves
The angels thronging in the trees
The Good News spread by willing feet
All running from the winding sheet
This broken world at last complete
A perfect day on Autumn street.

Whooper Swans: *or The Secret Gospel of Aengus and Yewberry*

Beaks dusted with the pollen
Of the Summer stars
Forms gilded by the halo of the Midnight Sun
Flying high above the lonely ice bear
They surf the bare back of the North wind
Feathered long ships with prows of gold
Wodin's storm rimmed trumpets
Creaking - whooping wanderers
From the Edda's glacial cold
Winging wearily past wave-lashed Lindisfarne
Where scratching swans-down feather's
Illumine inner journeys
The rush-lit transmigration of pure enlightened souls.

Oberon's Journey

They touch across an ancient glade
His Oak affords her Rowan shade
And in her turn the mountain maid
Protects him from the lightning blade
They grew together long ago
Across the river far below
And now - beneath their Bridge of Sighs
Their acorns and their berries glide
To form a bridal train of seeds
That flow wherever water leads
Down to a Greenwood far away
In which their laughing children play
Until the swallows - chasing flies
Migrate beneath late Summer skies
And duck bright swords of fledgling trees
A tunnel made of Greenwood leaves
Until the river - veiled from me
Beneath a snow-swept mystery
Elopes into the boundless sea
And sets their sylvan spirits free.

A Yeoman forecasts the history of 3 acorns

Inside the egg
Within its cup
A galleon creaks
Within this nut

And inside this one
As I shake
I feel a tithe barn taking shape

But this one here I'll leave alone
To grow for God and tend my bones.

On viewing gravestones at Earlham Road Cemetery, Norwich

It seems a crime that lives so rich
Are blessed with verse as trite as this

Now if I were a Christmas cracker
Such awful piffle wouldn't matter

But as I'm not I must protest
At drivel in a place of rest

I'd rather lie here undisturbed
Than be eternally perturbed
By such banality in words

So when I die will William McGonagall be
The bard they choose to pen my sweet obituary...?

No - when I die old friends must surely see

That - in some cardboard box
In some forgotten field
I rest beneath my acorns
Doggerel free.

Two Butterflies

"Each year"
The man said to the child
"My wife comes back as a butterfly
On the anniversary of her death
She flies through our bedroom window
And hangs like a silk shawl over my frozen memories."

The man has long since died
Years have passed by
But I often wonder if…
On the anniversary of her passing
Two admirals flutter gently through that melting window.

Uncle Jack: *For Mum. Read at the Graveside, May 2003*

Birdsong drifts through drifting mind
His eighty years of life unwinds
They monitor for vital signs
A seismograph of arcs and lines
He's waiting in the transit lounge
He's poised between the air and ground
The light for Heaven's turning green
In pulses on a plasma screen
He lived to see the World at War
He met his girl at 44
His life was spent erecting pumps
To drain The Empire's oily sumps
The industry he loved has died
They pulled it down in '85
He loved steam engines - smoking trains
The sanctity of country lanes
He loved the birds - he loved the trees
The Summer sound of droning bees
He was a man of modest dreams
Who sometimes lived beyond his means
He built things with his dextrous hands
He loved his wife - he loved this land
He loved his snooker - rugby - scotch
The ticking sound of whirling clocks
He loved his bikes - the Isle of Man
And Famous Grouse - the odd wee dram
He came to us when Elfie died
My mother kept his flame alive
He motored up for long weekends
In Nissans - not Mercedes Benz
He turned his hand to goldfish ponds
To bird tables and wind-chime songs
He went with mum to Tenerife
Enjoyed a decade's extra lease...
And now he lies upon this bed
A mass of tubes around his head
The light for Heaven's turning green
In pulses on a plasma screen
He's boarding soon to meet his wife
A curtain draws around this life
As on Earth then so Above
What will remain of Jack is Love...

Shield Shiefing's Last Journey: *Extracted from Beowulf - A free verse translation.*

"Listen
People of Denmark
You will have heard of the glory days of our Royal ancestors
You all know how they came by such gilded renown
Remember Shield Shiefing the hall shaker
And tumbler of mead benches
He who other sea wolves learned to approach with fear
Yet was sky-clad in childhood..?
He grew great none - the - less
Wyrd bright as the bears under the Northern Lights
Until all the people on surrounding shores
And over the whale road
Acknowledged his prowess with wonder
And gave him their fealty
Sea gold - frozen honey from the Baltic winter
Furs and the tusk of the sea unicorn
All the hard won treasures of our Northern fastness
He was loved and admired by all
Sound timbered heartwood of our seafaring people
Polestar at the helm of our dragon-prowed realm
And later he fathered a sea cub
Urchin before the mead hall - new star on the water
Sent by God who had watched our grief
The sorrow of those who knew Him not
Therefore the light bringer - wielder of life's flame
Allowed this spark to kindle
And soon many in the North took up Beow's name for their own litters
For he too was worthy of renown
Giving freely of himself
As should all those who wish to have friendship when danger draws about them
Such honour is bestowed only on those who do glorious deeds
When the Fates decreed Beow's father sailed out of this world
His company carrying him to the sea which surrounds us
For this was his death wish - this poet of battle
Father on earth to his stalwart people
Long lived keeper of his people's flame

His swan-necked boat - girdled with ice
Rode in the harbour - eager to take him
And his company laid him in her wooden womb
By the mast - as was their custom in this world
Then great treasure from far flung countries was heaped about him
Never was any ship more ready for the fray
Filled as it was with the glory of battle.
And they gave him death gifts for the journey
To aid him on his unknown passage - under star and over water
The treasure given was equal to the gifts given when he began life's journey
As a small child on a great ship venturing into the unknown
Then - high above him they hoisted his gold symbol
And in great sorrow gave him back to the ocean which had brought him
And not even the wisest know where the wild winds blew him
And who unshipped him at his journeys end."

The Whole of the Moon – A Prophecy
For Mike Scott and the Waterboys

"This is the song that I want them to sing
When my long ship is launched
In the teeth of the wind

This is the song that I want them to cry
As the flames of my soul
Lick the eaves of the sky

This is the song that I'll ask them to play
As the wind and the rain
Bear my strange boat away

For this is the song I will leave in your womb
As the child of my joy
Throws the ivory runes

And these are the words that will blaze on my tomb
That I saw the crescent
But you'll see the whole of the moon."

The Emperor's Embrace: *For Apsley Cherry Garrard*

Jesus spent forty days and nights
Tempted by starvation
And the Devil
The rain lashed the ark
For forty days and nights
This seems the Biblical equivalent
Of the ultimate privation
Yet the Emperor Penguin spends eighty days and nights
In the darkness of the world
Balancing an egg on his legs
And Englishmen came half way round the world
To spend forty days and nights
In search of such privation
If God cares for the earth
As much as the Emperor
For his egg
We too should be prepared to wait in darkness
On a sunless sea
Hoping against hope
Balancing the egg of faith
Pilgrims beneath a cloud of unknowing
Wrapped
Although we know not
In the wings of God's embrace.

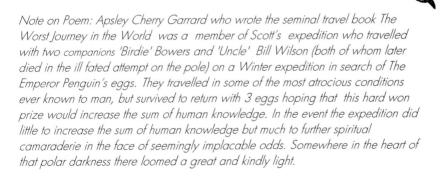

Note on Poem: Apsley Cherry Garrard who wrote the seminal travel book The Worst Journey in the World was a member of Scott's expedition who travelled with two companions 'Birdie' Bowers and 'Uncle' Bill Wilson (both of whom later died in the ill fated attempt on the pole) on a Winter expedition in search of The Emperor Penguin's eggs. They travelled in some of the most atrocious conditions ever known to man, but survived to return with 3 eggs hoping that this hard won prize would increase the sum of human knowledge. In the event the expedition did little to increase the sum of human knowledge but much to further spiritual camaraderie in the face of seemingly implacable odds. Somewhere in the heart of that polar darkness there loomed a great and kindly light.

Anam Cara: *Celtic Soul Friendship*

Interlaced by Celtic rings
We feel the joy that Nature brings
The roots of love are strong and deep
The fruits of love are ours to keep
And though we follow seasons round
And old leaves float down to the ground
We know that in our woodland souls
The cup of Spring will make us whole
For though the Winter weighs us down
We'll soon be wearing springtime crowns
And find that - though our trials be great
We'll meet beside the kissing gate
To walk back through another year
Our anam cara pure and clear.

Out Take: *Movie Madeleine*

I found you
Sliced
On the cutting room floor
My celluloid girl from years before
I picked you up
And spliced you in
Rewound my life
And pressed
Begin...

Epitaphs

An Epitaph for Ted Hughes

A great oak felled on a windswept moor
A Druid closing Summer's door
A salmon beached beneath a tor
The shape-shifter will shape no more.

An Epitaph for a.w. and his Lakeland Guides

The Prelude
Penned by God's surveyor
The Borough Treasurer of Nature.

Basho's Epitaph

Don't fish for poems
Nets of words
Come up empty.

The Man who nearly finished The Book of Kells
An apocryphal Irish Legend

Oozing from his goose quilled pen
A great river of gold
Washed the last Amen

And then he went outside to cry
And punch his fist at gold leafed sky

And then he went to have a drink
"It's done" he said... "The Kells in ink!"

He showed it proudly to the throng
Who'd waited 40 years for John
To come up with his vast swansong

Then Brother Michael softly said
His voice a lilting feather bed

"I hate to be a killjoy John
You've worked so hard to get this done

But isn't Jesus S not Z...?"

(Twas then the brother dropped down dead.)

249

Transmutation

The pain that leads me through the fire
Transmutes the lead of my desire
Till all desires are put on hold
The Fire of Love producing gold.

Swallows Know

Swallows know when it's time to go
But people seldom do

I thought there was going to be more to this poem
But swallows know when it's time to go
And poets seldom do...!

THE SWELLS OF THE BRIGHTON AQUARIUM VISIT THEIR FRIENDS AT THE ZOO.

Index

Virginia McKenna and Richard Bonfield at the Born Free Poetry Reading,
Born Free Headquarters, Horsham - July 30th 2009

Photograph by Mike Dooley ©2009

Born Free Foundation

Keep wildlife in the wild

The Born Free Foundation is a dynamic international wildlife charity, founded by Virginia McKenna and Bill Travers following their starring roles in the classic film *Born Free*. Today, led by their son Will Travers, Born Free takes action worldwide for wild animal welfare and compassionate conservation. From small beginnings, Born Free has grown into a global force for wildlife.

Born Free believes wildlife belongs in the wild and works to phase out zoos and stop captive animal exploitation. We rescue individuals from tiny cages and give them lifetime care in spacious sanctuaries. Born Free protects threatened species in their natural habitat, working with local communities to help people and wildlife live together without conflict. Find out more and get involved at www.bornfree.org.uk

Zoo Check

Zoo Check is at the heart of Born Free and works globally to stop captive animal suffering and phase-out zoos. Millions of animals suffer in zoos, circuses, marine parks and for tourists' photos. Born Free challenges the multi-billion-pound zoo industry, exposes neglect and fights cruelty, campaigns for tighter legislation, publishes ground-breaking reports, and stops animal exploitation in advertising, TV and films. Our Travellers Animal Alert campaign works with the travel industry and tourists to stop captive animal exploitation. Born Free co-ordinates the ENDCAP coalition linking animal welfare groups throughout Europe to END CAPtive animal suffering.

Elephants

Born Free's Elephants project protects wild elephants and their habitat in Africa and Asia and campaigns against exploitation. Born Free fights the brutal ivory trade worldwide; funds anti-poaching patrols in Kenya, Tanzania, Zambia, Mali and Sierra Leone; resolves conflict between people and elephants; relocates threatened elephants to places of safety; cares for orphan baby elephants in Sri Lanka; opposes the capture of wild elephants for zoos; and exposes the plight of captive elephants.

Big Cats

Born Free's Big Cat project is dedicated to protecting big cats. Born Free rescues lions, leopards, tigers and cheetahs from tiny cages and gives them lifetime care at our sanctuaries in South Africa, India and soon Ethiopia; operates a major tiger conservation initiative in India and protects wild lions in Africa; campaigns to end hunting lions and leopards for 'sport'; and develops humane solutions when people and big cats come in conflict.

Great apes

Born Free's Primate project is dedicated to protecting great apes and monkeys. The project helped develop GRASP, the UN's Great Ape Survival Project; fights the global trade in ape 'bushmeat' and exotic pets; cares for orphan apes at sanctuaries in Cameroon and Uganda; funds rare gorilla conservation in the Democratic Republic of Congo; rescues baboons and vervet monkeys in Malawi and Zambia and returns them to the wild.

Wolves

Born Free's Wolf project works to protect wolves around the world. In a major initiative, Born Free protects the Ethiopian wolf - the world's rarest canid; develops humane solutions when wolves come in conflict with people; campaigns against trophy hunting of wolves; investigates and exposes the plight of captive wolves.

Bears

Born Free's Bear project helps protect bears across the world. Born Free investigates how tourists affect polar bear behaviour and encourages good practice in Canada; rescues orphan polar bear cubs and returns them to the wild; tackles bear killing for gallbladders for Asian medicines in North America; helps rescue bears from bile farms in China and Vietnam and campaigns to end the exploitation of bears in zoos and circuses.

Marine

Our Marine project protects key ocean-living creatures under threat. Born Free funds endangered marine turtle, whale shark and dugong conservation in Tanzania; monitors and safeguards wild orcas in Canada; protects rare marine turtles in Indonesia and supports action against illegal trade in eggs and adult animals; helps rescue stranded marine mammals in the UK; fights captive cetacean exploitation; and opposes wild capture of dolphins and whales for marine parks.

Global Friends

Through our Global Friends project Born Free works with local communities to find compassionate solutions so people and wildlife can live together without conflict. Our educational activities inspire young and old alike to learn about and respect the wild, and provides schools with vital resources in Kenya, Ethiopia, Uganda, Tanzania, South Africa, Democratic Republic of Congo and Sri Lanka.

Global initiatives

But our work doesn't stop there. Born Free responds to emergency situations worldwide, participates in international coalitions such as the Species Survival Network, operates the People & Wildlife project with Oxford University's WildCRU* department, and much, much more. Today Born Free employs 35 staff in the UK, and supports more than 100 field workers and consultants in over 15 countries around the world. Born Free has branches in Kenya and Ethiopia, plus an affiliate organisation in the USA.

*Wildlife Conservation Research Unit

To find out more about Born Free visit www.bornfree.org.uk

Keep wildlife in the wild

Go wild with Born Free!

There are lots of ways to get involved:

Join Born Free today

Become a member. You'll support animal care and conservation, get a great gift pack *and* colour magazines.

Choose from:

- **Exclusive Platinum (£6.50/mth)** - give extra support to ALL our major projects (Zoo Check, Big Cats, Elephants, Primate, Marine, Wolves and Bears).

- **Special Gold (£3.25/mth)** - give extra support to ONE project (listed above).

- **Silver (£2.50/mth)** - give general support.

Plus WildCrew our club for **wild kids (8-12 yrs, £1/mth)** or **teens (13-16 yrs, £1.50/mth)**. Includes joining pack and regular mini-mags.

Call 01403 240170 or visit www.bornfree.org.uk quoting RB2010.

Adopt your own animal

Makes a unique present for someone special! Includes personalised gift pack and updates for just £30. Help look after your animal and safeguard their species in the wild. Choose from:

1. Roque the tiger

Roque ('Rocky') was a tiny cub when taken from his mother and put on sale in a Spanish pet-shop. We rescued the scared cub and today this magnificent tiger lives in a jungle enclosure at our sanctuary in India. He'll always rely on us. So please help provide his daily food and care.

2. Emily Kate the African elephant

Emily Kate is a wild elephant, a young member of the famous EB family. They live in Amboseli National Park, Kenya. Emily Kate is independent and feisty, named by our patron Martin Clunes after his own young daughter. Adopt Emily Kate and help keep her safe from ivory poachers.

3. Afrika the little chimp

Afrika was just a few months old when her mother was killed by poachers. The terrified baby was kept in a tiny cage, filthy and starving. Luckily she was rescued and has now recovered at a special sanctuary in Uganda. Adopt little Afrika and help fund her daily food and care.

Gift pack

- Personalised certificate
- Stand-up photo-portrait (14.5 x 20cm) of your animal
- Adoption papers with your animal's full story
- Notebook featuring your animal
- Updates about your animal in spring & autumn
- Born Free window sticker
- Glossy Born Free folder

Your adoption will last for one year.

To adopt call 01403 240170, or visit bornfree.org.uk

So much more!

There are many other ways to go wild with Born Free. Make a regular donation, sign up for our free monthly e-news bulletins, choose from a wild range of wildlife gifts and merchandise, or join Activate – our letter-writing team of arm-chair campaigners!

Just call 01403 240170 or visit www.bornfree.org.uk

Born Free Foundation
3 Grove House
Foundry Lane
Horsham RH13 5PL
info@bornfree.org.uk
01403 240170
bornfree.org.uk
Reg Charity No: 1070906

Keep wildlife in the wild

The Born Free Alphabet: *For Virginia McKenna, Will Travers , the Born Free Team and children everywhere*

"What were zoos...?" said the child
"They were acres of steel sorrow" said the mother
"Where tigers roamed their dirty pens
Great carnivores as battery hens
Their blazing beauty tiger-striped
Washed out by cheap fluorescent lights."
"And what were circuses ?" said the child
"They were animal freak-shows" said the father
"Where lions... natural instincts chained
Were made to leap through hoops of flame
Where elephants were made to sit
And beg the clowns for bags of crisps."
"And what were dolphinariums...?" said the child
"They were chlorine coliseums" said the mother
"Where the oceans most translucent jewels
Were made to jump wires in a swimming pool
A choreography of shame
For which we all must take the blame."
"And where have they gone...?" said the child
"We fought for years to close them down" said the father
To exorcize the dreadful stain
That caused the wild things so much pain
And now the zoos are all extinct
The bullrings turned to skating rinks
And all the centuries of pain
Are bathed in loves eternal flame.
And all the animals are free
To skim across the azure seas
To stalk across the ancient plains
To dance in gardens wet with rain.
The jungles all have been replanted
Their green mansions all re-enchanted
And now the trees have all re-grown

The tigers claim their ancient thrones.
The lion - still the king of beasts
On teeming plains has been released
The elephants in herds all roam
Across their lovely hosepipe homes
And dolphins surf the coral seas
With smiles that say... We're all born free...!
"You saved the Earth" said the child... *"you fought so hard*
The contents of the ark are ours...!"
"Can we go on safari sometime" said the child
"And learn the Born Free Alphabet...?"
"Of course" said the mother and father... "This is your prize...!"
Then they switched on the light in their daughter's eyes.

Richard Bonfield c July 2009

Painting by Pollyanna Pickering

The Poet

Richard Bonfield was born in Leicester on the 27th of April 1959: Taurus with Sagittarius rising, the moon in Capricorn and Scorpio mid-heaven. He shares his birthday with the former poet laureate Cecil Day Lewis.

His first experience of poetry came when, at the tender age of 5 his father gave him a beautiful miniature edition of the Rubaiyat of Omar Khayyam in the famous Fitzgerald translation which has hooked him in a noose of poetic light ever since. The book, which still sits in his bookcase is beautifully illustrated with watercolour washes of Arabia and this conjunction of poetry and art has informed all his subsequent work.

Richard was educated at Wyggeston Boys' Grammar School in Leicester, following in the illustrious footsteps of Richard and David Attenborough, where he was subliminally influenced by the hurricane of words that is Ted Hughes. Then, for want of something better to do he went up to The University of East Anglia to take an Honours Degree in Development Studies in 1977.

In 1989 he went on the Enterprise Allowance Scheme as a writer and it was during this period that he wrote a column entitled The Social Incompetent's Handbook for The Truth edited by Cover's former editor Steve Caplin which was syndicated through W.H. Smith to a wildly appreciative audience countrywide

At the age of 30 and rapidly going nowhere, busily doing nothing he wrote his first proper poem 'First Fire' whilst cat-napping by the autumnal wood burner in his marvellous, if draughty Victorian flat and the rest - as they say is a complete mystery as, over the subsequent 20 years he has had some 300 different poems published in over 30 magazines countrywide .

Last year he was honoured to accept Virginia McKenna's invitation to become Poet in Residence for the Born Free Foundation and is delighted that Animated Nature is supporting their wonderful work

Richard's interests include the Natural World in all its manifestations, Egyptology, Nordic mythology and the interface between science and religion. He is also a fervent disciple of The Perennial Philosophy i.e. the belief that, at the highest level all the great mystics of the world's religions are basically singing from the same hymn sheet or as Rumi the famous Persian poet and philosopher wrote in more decorous language

"The lamps may be different but the light is the same."

As far as his own religion is concerned he would I think describe himself as a Vegetarian Christian Druid with extreme pantheistic tendencies…!

Since returning to the city of his birth a decade ago Richard has worked for ASDA, firstly as a Beers, Wines and Spirits colleague, where he became a much appreciated wine guru and more recently as a grocery colleague. He is a popular member of the team at ASDA, Oadby where he is always "Happy to help"!

Since completing Animated Nature Richard has been busy working on his next collection provisionally entitled The Green Man's Almanack which is intended as a companion piece for Swan for all Seasons.